10

MINUTE GUIDE TO

ANNUAL REPORTS AND PROSPECTUSES

by Eric Gelb, CPA, MBA

alpha
books
Macmillan Spectrum/Alpha

A Division of Macmillan General Reference
A Simon & Schuster Macmillan Company
1633 Broadway, New York, NY 10019-6785

International Standard Book Number: 0-02-861116-0
Library of Congress Catalog Card Number: 96-068551

98 97 96   8 7 6 5 4 3 2 1

Interpretation of the printing code: the rightmost double-digit number is the year of the book's first printing; the rightmost single-digit number is the number of the book's printing. For example, a printing code of 96-1 shows that this copy of the book was printed during the first printing of the book in 1996.

Printed in the United States of America

Publisher: Theresa Murtha

Development Editor: Debra W. Englander

Production Editor: Michael Thomas

Copy Editor: Linda Seifert

Technical Editor: Mark Merryweather, BDO Seidman, LLP

Cover Designer: Dan Armstrong

Designer: Kim Scott

Indexer: Debra Myers

Production Team: Heather Butler, Angela Calvert, Scott Tullis, Megan Wade, Christy Wagner, Kelly Warner

CONTENTS

Introduction

If you've ever gone grocery shopping, you know that labels help you determine whether a particular product is worth buying. The same is true for investing. And to become an educated investor, you must read the company's "labels"—namely, their annual reports and prospectuses.

As with any diet, annual reports and prospectuses should be used as a part of a balanced diet of investor information—some provided by the company and some provided by third-party sources such as the media. With any label, the listing may be incomplete and in some cases misleading. Company information, especially the financial statements contained in annual reports and prospectuses, is historical information about the company because these statements reflect the company's financial results for a prior period. And past results do not guarantee future performance.

About This Guide

Companies prepare annual reports and prospectuses to provide you with some of the information you need to make more prudent investment decisions. The purpose of this guide is to explain, in easy-to-read language, how to read, interpret, and analyze annual reports and prospectuses. If you've never read—much less understood—either of these financial documents, then this guide is a good place to start. In addition, this book can be a refresher for more experienced investors.

The *10 Minute Guide to Annual Reports and Prospectuses* contains 32 lessons, each explaining some aspect of financial reporting. Because each lesson builds on previous lessons, you should read each chapter in numerical order. Each chapter should take no longer than 10 minutes to complete.

CONVENTIONS USED IN THIS BOOK

Before you begin, note that the *10 Minute Guide to Annual Reports and Prospectuses* uses the following icons to help you understand key terms and concepts:

Plain English   Defines new or unfamiliar terms in (you got it) "plain English."

Panic Button   Identifies potential trouble areas and offers practical solutions.

Investor Insight   Highlights useful ideas that help you make better investing decisions and may also help you save time and avoid confusion.

DEDICATION

To Mildred Goldstein—my special grandma. Thank you for your love and kindness and all the wonderful things you showed me.

GETTING STARTED

In this lesson, you gain an overview of the information found in annual reports, and learn how to use this information when making investment decisions.

KNOWLEDGE IS POWER

The key to making sound investment decisions is to collect and interpret as much information about an industry and company as possible. Fortunately, annual reports and prospectuses provide a solid background. To the unseasoned investor, company documents may be intimidating at first glance. However, after you become familiar with the jargon published in annual reports and prospectuses, you'll be able to read these materials easily.

RESEARCHING COMPANIES

If you're looking for information on an American company, you can find detailed and expansive resources, many of which are right at your fingertips, many at your public library, and some in your living room. These include newspapers, financial talk shows, newsletters, magazines, brokers' and analysts' reports and recommended lists, companies' own investor relations departments and Web sites, and on-line computer news services. The Securities and Exchange Commission (SEC) also has a Web site and allows people to download all EDGAR filings directly.

These sources of information provide up-to-date information and therefore enable users to update, supplement, and enhance the information contained in annual reports and prospectuses. As time goes by and more information becomes available, you can make more informed investment decisions.

 Annual Report   An annual report is a document that presents and explains a company's business activities for the most recent twelve-month operating period. It is important to keep in mind that companies publish financial reports after the end of the relevant period.

 Prospectus   A prospectus is a document that describes the terms and conditions associated with the offering of new securities. Much of the information contained in a prospectus is similar to that found in an annual report, except that companies issue prospectuses whenever they issue stocks, bonds, or mutual funds.

UNRAVELING A MYSTERY

Exploring an annual report or prospectus is like reading a mystery novel. You want to learn about a company's health, gain insight into its business operations and finances, and ultimately assess its potential for growth. You try to uncover clues that might signal impending opportunities or problems. After studying and digesting a company's annual report and prospectus, coupled with additional up-to-date information, you may be in a better position to assess whether the investment's potential return is worth the risk, or whether you should move on to another prospect.

In this lesson, you gained an overview of the information in annual reports and prospectuses and the purposes of these reports. In the next lesson, you learn about important terms in the documents you'll use to research an investment.

IMPORTANT INVESTMENT CONCEPTS AND DOCUMENTS

In this lesson, you learn about some of the key documents that you'll see when researching a particular company.

ACCOUNTING PERIOD

The accounting period is a time frame in which to measure the company's financial results. In the annual report, companies report financial information on a 12-month basis.

 Fiscal Year   A fiscal year (FY) is the 12-month period during which a company measures its operations, and at the end of which a profit or loss is determined.

Often, a company's fiscal year does not coincide with the calendar year. One example is a seasonal business, such as an outdoor stadium. For a seasonal company, a fiscal year may begin on October 1 and end September 30, so that the year-end figures reflect the company after its major or peak business activity has occured—in its most liquid condition.

FORMS 10-K, 8-K, AND 10-Q

Form 10-K contains information that is similar to the annual report, but may contain more detail than the annual report. Additional information typically includes management's detailed discussion of the company's financial position and results of operations, management, compensation, and litigation.

> **Form 10-K** Form 10-K is required of companies listed on a U.S. stock exchange and is the format an annual report takes when it is filed with the SEC. Form 10-K contains information not only required to be published under GAAP, but also additional information required by the SEC as a condition of being listed on the stock exchange.

The Securities and Exchange Commission (SEC), formed under the Securities Act of 1934, is a U.S. Federal agency that oversees U.S. Securities laws. The SEC requires publicly traded companies to file a Form 10-K within 90 days of the company's fiscal year end. Once filed with the SEC, Form 10-K becomes public information. When researching a company, you should request the annual report and a 10-K if it was published separately. Read both documents closely.

The cover of a 10-K contains the company's name and address. Form 10-K includes information similar to the annual report, but contains more details as required by the SEC. Such information includes a discussion of the company's general business practices, the company's markets, properties, employees, transactions, legal proceedings, environmental liabilities, executive compensation, and directors and officers.

The last pages of a Form 10-K typically list an index of exhibits, including a list of Form 8-K filings. Exhibits are other events and occurrences the company is required to list, but for which the company doesn't have to include the actual reports.

 Form 8-K   Form 8-K is used to explain significant changes or events that might affect the company, its financial situation, or security holders.

The SEC requires publicly held companies to file a Form 8-K within 15 days of most material changes and within 5 days of certain changes. Material changes can involve events concerning corporate bylaws, executive compensation, financing agreements, changes in control, bankruptcy, resignation of directors, and merger and acquisition activity.

Form 10-Q   Form 10-Q reports a company's quarterly results. The information contained in a 10-Q is similar to that contained in a 10-K, but is less detailed and is unaudited.

The SEC requires publicly traded companies to file a Form 10-Q within 45 days of the end of the company's quarter. A 10-Q is required only for each of the first three quarters of the fiscal year; the fourth quarter information is included in Form 10-K. Form 10-Q and quarterly financial reports are not normally audited by the company's independent auditors; rather, they are often reviewed by the independent auditors.

Proxy Statement   A statement sent to shareholders by management to solicit votes on issues that will be discussed at the annual shareholder meeting. The form invites common shareholders to vote by mail or give their votes to another person to use on their behalf.

The SEC requires companies to provide shareholders who vote by proxy with information before a vote on company matters is held. A proxy statement often contains information about proposed management compensation plans, election of directors, appointment of independent auditors, merger and acquisition activities, and resolutions.

Read Proxy Statements   Read all proxy statements, as they may contain important information that affects the company's future and are not included in an annual report or Form 10-K.

AUDITOR'S OPINION

Publicly traded companies are required to have their annual financial statements audited by an independent public accounting firm. Independent auditors offer an *opinion* about the company's financial statements that relates to the financial statements included in the annual report. The auditor's opinion is discussed in Lesson 23.

In this lesson, you learned about Form 10-K, Form 8-K, Form 10-Q, and auditor's opinions. In the next lesson, you learn about the financial statements that appear in annual reports and prospectuses.

3

INGREDIENTS IN ANNUAL REPORTS AND PROSPECTUSES

In this lesson, you learn about the financial statements that appear in annual reports and prospectuses.

COMPANY OVERVIEW AND HIGHLIGHTS

The first pages of an annual report summarize a company's activities during the latest 12-month operating period. Figures on sales, income, earnings per share, return on equity, leverage, and capital expenditures are included. Financial data covering 2–5 years may be presented in a table or bar graph. Highlights may include positive activities such as the launch of new products, entry into new markets, business acquisitions, restructurings, and changes in top management.

 Spin Doctors Despite the rules regarding disclosure and presentation of information, text written by the company almost always portrays the company in the most favorable light. Maintain a healthy sense of skepticism as you read.

MANAGEMENT DISCUSSION

Annual reports contain a management discussion and analysis of the company's financials which must comply with SEC and accounting rules. There is also a "Letter to Shareholders," in which the chairman or president can discuss whatever he or she wants. (See Intel Corporation's 1995 Management's letter on the next page.)

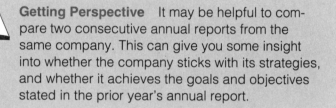

Getting Perspective It may be helpful to compare two consecutive annual reports from the same company. This can give you some insight into whether the company sticks with its strategies, and whether it achieves the goals and objectives stated in the prior year's annual report.

THE BALANCE SHEET

A balance sheet (such as Intel Corporation's consolidated balance sheet shown following) reports the company's financial position as of the last day of a company's fiscal year or quarter.

Accountants often describe the balance sheet as a company "snapshot" because the data reflects a given operation in terms of dollars and cents for one specific moment in time. Major categories on the balance sheet are assets, liabilities, and owner's equity. You'll learn more about the information in a balance sheet in Lesson 12.

To Our Stockholders
We are happy to report our sixth consecutive year of both record revenues and earnings per share.

Revenues totaled $16.2 billion, up 41 percent from $11.5 billion in 1994. Earnings per share rose 54 percent over last year, to $4.03.

Our strong performance in 1995 was rooted in growing demand for PCs based on our Pentium® processors. The PC market continued its remarkable growth, with approximately 60 million PCs sold worldwide this year, up about 25 percent from 1994.

We were pleased to see the increased popularity of the Internet and other communications applications this year. In particular, we are very excited by the opportunities represented by the booming World Wide Web. With more than 180 million units in use worldwide, PCs are the predominant gateway to the World Wide Web. We believe that this easy-to-use, graphically based Internet interface will continue to attract new users and investments in the PC communications world, helping to expand the PC's role as a consumer communications device and driving future PC sales.

At Intel, our most important job is to make high-performance microprocessors for the computing industry. To do this, we follow four basic strategies:

3. Remove barriers to technology flow. We believe that if computers work better, do more and are easier to use, more PCs will be sold and more Intel processors will be needed. We therefore work with other industry leaders to develop new PC technologies, such as the PCI "bus," which has been widely adopted. This technology removes bottlenecks to provide greatly enhanced graphics capabilities. We incorporate our chips into PCI building blocks, such as PC motherboards, to help computer manufacturers bring their products to market faster. We also work closely with software developers to help create rich applications, such as PC video conferencing and animated 3D Web sites, that make the most of the power of Intel processors.

4. Promote the Intel brand. We continue to invest in education and marketing programs that describe the benefits of genuine Intel technology. Our Intel Inside® program expanded in 1995 to include broadcast advertising. Hundreds of OEMs worldwide are participating to let users know that there are genuine Intel microprocessors inside their PCs.

New PC communications applications and emerging markets

1. Develop products quickly. We try to bring new technology to the market as quickly as possible. In 1995, we introduced the new high-end Pentium® Pro processor. This came less than three years after the introduction of the Pentium processor, which is now the processor of choice in the mainstream PC market. Together, these products provide computer buyers with a wide spectrum of computing choices.

2. Invest in manufacturing. We believe Intel's state-of-the-art chip manufacturing facilities are the best in the industry. We spent $3.6 billion on capital in 1995, up 45 percent from 1994. These heavy investments are paying off: in 1995, we were able to bring our new 0.35-micron manufacturing process into production months earlier than originally planned. Our newest facility, the most advanced in the microprocessor industry, makes our highest speed Pentium and Pentium Pro processors. In the end, these investments benefit PC buyers directly in the form of more powerful, less expensive computing options.

Beyond our primary task of making microprocessors, we invest in a range of computing and communications applications that support our core business. Our supercomputer and network server efforts take advantage of the flexibility and power of the Intel architecture, while our flash memory business supports booming communications applications such as cellular phones. These product areas are detailed on the following pages.

Overall, our focused strategies have kept us on the right track. Of course, we continue to attract competition, both from makers of software-compatible microprocessors and from makers of alternative-architecture chips. We will try to stay nimble to maintain our position in the industry.

This is a particularly exciting time to be in the computing industry. New applications like the Internet are driving increased demand for computers, and emerging markets around the world are quickly adopting the latest computer technology. We look forward to meeting the challenges of this business as the computer's role continues to expand.

GORDON E. MOORE
Chairman

ANDREW S. GROVE
President and
Chief Executive Officer

CRAIG R. BARRETT
Executive Vice President and
Chief Operating Officer

INTEL CORPORATION 1996

Consolidated Balance Sheets

December 30, 1995 and December 31, 1994

(In millions—except per share amounts)	1995	1994
Assets		
Current assets:		
Cash and cash equivalents	$ 1,463	$ 1,180
Short-term investments	995	1,230
Accounts receivable, net of allowance for doubtful accounts of $57 ($32 in 1994)	3,116	1,978
Inventories	2,004	1,169
Deferred tax assets	408	552
Other current assets	111	58
Total current assets	8,097	6,167
Property, plant and equipment:		
Land and buildings	3,145	2,292
Machinery and equipment	7,099	5,374
Construction in progress	1,548	850
	11,792	8,516
Less accumulated depreciation	4,321	3,149
Property, plant and equipment, net	7,471	5,367
Long-term investments	1,653	2,127
Other assets	283	155
Total assets	$ 17,504	$ 13,816
Liabilities and stockholders' equity		
Current liabilities:		
Short-term debt	$ 346	$ 517
Accounts payable	864	575
Deferred income on shipments to distributors	304	269
Accrued compensation and benefits	758	588
Accrued advertising	218	108
Other accrued liabilities	328	538
Income taxes payable	801	429
Total current liabilities	3,619	3,024
Long-term debt	400	392
Deferred tax liabilities	620	389
Put warrants	725	744
Commitments and contingencies		
Stockholders' equity:		
Preferred Stock, $.001 par value, 50 shares authorized; none issued	—	—
Common Stock, $.001 par value, 1,400 shares authorized; 821 issued and outstanding in 1995 (827 in 1994) and capital in excess of par value	2,583	2,306
Retained earnings	9,557	6,961
Total stockholders' equity	12,140	9,267
Total liabilities and stockholders' equity	$ 17,504	$ 13,816

See accompanying notes.

Reprinted by permission of Intel Corporation, copyright 1996 Intel Corporation.

THE INCOME STATEMENT

The income statement reports the company's business activity for a particular fiscal year or quarter. The Coca-Cola Company's 1995 consolidated income statement (below) shows sales of $18 billion compared to 1994 sales of $16 billion.

Income statements reflect the dollar value of the products a company has sold during the period, less the costs and expenses related to those sales. The difference between sales and expenses equals net income (profit) or loss.

The Coca-Cola Company and Subsidiaries

Consolidated Statements of Income

Year Ended December 31, *(In millions except per share data)*	1995	1994	1993
Net Operating Revenues	**$ 18,018**	$ 16,181	$ 13,963
Cost of goods sold	**6,940**	6,168	5,160
Gross Profit	**11,078**	10,013	8,803
Selling, administrative and general expenses	**6,986**	6,297	5,695
Operating Income	**4,092**	3,716	3,108
Interest income	**245**	181	144
Interest expense	**272**	199	168
Equity income	**169**	134	91
Other income (deductions)-net	**20**	(104)	(2)
Gain on issuance of stock by Coca-Cola Amatil	**74**	—	12
Income before Income Taxes and **Change in Accounting Principle**	**4,328**	3,728	3,185
Income taxes	**1,342**	1,174	997
Income before Change in Accounting Principle	**2,986**	2,554	2,188
Transition effect of change in accounting for postemployment benefits	**—**	—	(12)
Net Income	**$ 2,986**	$ 2,554	$ 2,176
Income per Share			
Before change in accounting principle	**$ 2.37**	$ 1.98	$ 1.68
Transition effect of change in accounting for postemployment benefits	**—**	—	(.01)
Net Income per Share	**$ 2.37**	$ 1.98	$ 1.67
Average Shares Outstanding	**1,262**	1,290	1,302

See Notes to Consolidated Financial Statements.

Reprinted by permission of The Coca-Cola Company, copyright 1996 The Coca-Cola Company.

THE STATEMENT OF CASH FLOWS

A statement of cash flows reflects whether a company's business activity has produced cash or not, and reconciles two consecutive balance sheets in terms of cash amounts. The statement of cash flows shows how the company generated and used cash and is discussed in Lesson 31.

STATEMENT OF SHAREHOLDERS' EQUITY

The statement of shareholders' equity explains the changes in the owners' equity accounts. Changes include net income or loss, dividends paid to shareholders, and stock issued or retired. This statement also shows the changes in book value.

NOTES AND FOOTNOTES

Notes and footnotes are an important part of the company's financial statements and explain the balance sheet and income statement accounts, or explain how the amounts were computed. Footnotes provide important background information about what has happened to the company and help you make an assessment of the company's prospects. Footnotes are discussed in Lesson 21.

REPORT OF MANAGEMENT

The annual report includes a letter from management stating that management takes responsibility for the financial statements and confirming that it has examined the company's system of internal controls that is designed to prevent or detect material errors or irregularities in the financial statements in a timely manner. Unfortunately, even the most comprehensive system of internal controls is not foolproof.

GOING FURTHER BACK IN TIME

Company data over a five- or ten-year period may be useful for analyzing a company's longer-term past performance record and spotting company trends. These financial summaries include the key figures from the balance sheets and income statements for the relevant years.

SEGMENT INFORMATION

Many companies operate different businesses or different lines of business, so they also present information by industry segment.

Companies report segment information when:

- Segment sales revenues exceed 10 percent of the company's total revenues

- Segment operating profit or loss exceeds 10 percent of the company's total profit or loss

- Segment assets exceed 10 percent of the company's total assets

Segment information reported generally includes identifiable assets, sales, operating profit or loss, interest income and expense, depreciation, and capital expenditures.

Companies also report segment information by geographic region, especially if they sell their products overseas. Geographic segment information is typically provided when geographic sales exceed 10 percent of the company's total sales, and geographic operating profit or loss exceeds 10 percent of the company's total operating profit or loss.

 **Seeking Strengths and Weaknesses**   Segment information provides insight into how the company is developing its business. Are the financial results improving over time? Which segment is making a profit? Is their business expanding?

ACTION PHOTOS

To convey a sense of excitement and activity, companies usually include color photographs in their annual reports. Photos often portray new or profitable products, employees, management, the board of directors, key projects, awards, and facilities. You should view such artwork as company advertisements.

In this lesson, you learned more about the ingredients of annual reports. In the next lesson, you learn about mutual fund annual reports.

MUTUAL FUND ANNUAL REPORTS

In this lesson, you learn about mutual fund annual reports.

DEVELOPMENTS IN INVESTMENT CHOICES

Over the past two decades, mutual funds have revolutionized the way Americans invest their money. More money today is invested in mutual funds because they offer investors immediate diversification and professional money management.

A *mutual fund* is a pool of investor money managed by a mutual fund company with a particular objective. Each mutual fund has at least one fund manager who uses the investors' money to purchase stocks, bonds, commodities, or money market securities. Investments must be made in accordance with the fund's charter, which is spelled out in the fund prospectus. Mutual funds pose varying degrees of risk and may invest aggressively, conservatively, or somewhere in-between.

TWO REPORTS A YEAR

Mutual funds typically issue two financial reports a year—the semiannual report, which is often dated June 30 or April 30, and the year-end or annual report, which is often dated December 31 or October 31. With most funds, the midyear report and quarterly reports, if any have been issued, are not audited. The annual report is usually audited by a fund's independent auditor and includes the auditor's opinion.

Shareholder Letter   A shareholder letter is usually written by the fund's president or investment manager, and reviews the fund's investment objectives and performance for the current period.

In the shareholder letter, the manager may compare a fund's performance to an industry benchmark. For example, if the mutual fund invests in "blue chip" common stocks, the manager may compare the fund's performance to the Standard & Poor's (S&P) 500 Index. Did the fund's return beat the benchmark?

Standard & Poor's (S&P) 500 Index   The S&P 500 Index is a broad measure of changes in the stock market based on the average performance of 500 widely held common stocks.

CHARTS AND GRAPHS

Many mutual fund reports include charts and graphs. A line graph may compare the growth of a $10,000 investment in the fund to the growth of similar investments over five years, ten years, or over the life of the fund.

Pie chart graphs are used to show the percentage of each type of investment in the fund: common stocks, bonds, and cash; and the industry composition of the portfolio: utilities, consumer, and so on. Many reports include the fund's Net Asset Value (NAV) on a year-by-year basis and the fund's total return.

Net Asset Value (NAV)   NAV is each mutual fund share's portion of the value of the mutual fund's investments as calculated by the mutual fund at the end of each business day. The NAV is published in most major newspapers.

Top 10   By looking at a mutual fund's top 10 holdings, you'll get a sense of the type of investments in the portfolio and the degree to which the fund meets your investment objectives. Similarly, study the industry composition of the portfolio—the percent of the fund's asset that is invested in a particular industry.

PORTFOLIO

Some mutual fund financial reports include a more in-depth discussion of the fund's performance for the period than the shareholder's letter.

Depending on the investment objective of the fund, and the performance of the fund's investments, the value of the fund's common stock and bond investments may decline in a down market, and the fund's NAV will also decline.

Investment Portfolio An investment portfolio comprises the assets (securities) held within a mutual fund.

 Portfolio Turnover Portfolio turnover is the percentage of the portfolio's investments that are bought and sold in one year. A fund with a portfolio turnover rate of 100 percent means they effectively bought and sold every security in the portfolio.

Many mutual fund annual reports disclose annual portfolio turnover. If not, contact the fund's shareholder services line.

Beware of High Portfolio Turnover High portfolio turnover increases transaction expenses and often reduces your rate of return. Generally, mutual funds whose objective is to achieve aggressive growth experience higher portfolio turnover—in many cases, in excess of 100 percent.

STATEMENT OF ASSETS AND LIABILITIES

A mutual fund's statement of assets and liabilities reflects the fund's financial position at the stock or bond market's close on the date of the report. Assets typically include investments that are valued at market on the financial statement date. Other assets include collateral held for securities loaned and receivables. Two examples are dividends and interest income receivable, which represent income earned by the fund but not yet collected in cash.

Liabilities primarily represent amounts the fund owes for the purchase of new securities.

FOOTNOTES TO THE FINANCIAL STATEMENTS

Mutual fund financial reports include footnotes similar to those found in other annual reports. Footnotes include significant accounting policies, and related party and affiliate transactions.

SIGNIFICANT ACCOUNTING POLICIES

For mutual funds, significant accounting policies typically include security valuation, securities sold short, securities transactions and investment income, distributions of dividends and gains to shareholders, and federal income taxes.

RELATED PARTY AND AFFILIATE TRANSACTIONS

Related party and affiliate transactions typically include three types of transactions. The first type occurs when payment of fees is made to portfolio managers and financial advisors. The second occurs when a mutual fund accumulates an ownership stake of at least 5 percent of the company (this is called investment in affiliates). The third occurs when one mutual fund sells some of its investments to another mutual fund sponsored by the same mutual fund family.

In this lesson, you learned about mutual fund annual reports. In the next lesson, you learn about the contents of a prospectus associated with new securities.

Prospectuses— Explaining New Securities

In this lesson, you learn about the contents of a prospectus associated with the issuance of new securities.

Explaining New Securities

A prospectus describes the characteristics and risks associated with the offering of a publicly traded security or mutual fund. Prospectuses contain information similar to annual reports. However, prospectuses also contain key details and topics essential for an investor to make an informed investment decision about the new security. This includes risk factors and other matters that would otherwise have been covered by 10-K supplements and 8-Ks, which are not addressed in annual reports.

Front Cover

The front cover of the prospectus lists the dollar amount of the security, the number of shares or units offered, the issuer, and the type of security.

Other text on the front cover includes a summary description of the securities, the stated interest rate or dividend, when interest or dividends are payable, the maturity date, and whether and when the company can call (repurchase or retire) the security.

Highlighting Disclaimer

The front cover contains a boldface notation cautioning you to see the "risk factors" section. This section discusses what could go wrong with the company issuing the security. You also find a disclaimer stating that "these securities have not been approved or disapproved by the SEC or any other state securities commission." This means the SEC is not recommending the security and you must make your own independent investment decision.

 Invest in What You Know When you don't understand a company, how it makes money, or the nature, complexity, and terms of a security being offered, don't invest your money.

The Offering

This section of the prospectus explains the securities being offered for sale. In the case of fixed-income securities, including notes and bonds, the offering information includes the notes, the principal amount, the interest rate, the maturity date, interest payment dates, and the company's optional redemption or call rights.

Terms and conditions can include:

- Change of control provisions that require the company to prepay the notes or redeem the security in the event the issuer is acquired by another company

- Asset sale proceeds in the event the company sells assets in excess of a certain dollar amount

- Guarantees of the security. Debt obligations may be guaranteed by the company

- The notes' ranking. *Ranking* means in the event of a competing claim where the securities stand with respect to the company's other outstanding securities (obligations)

The offering may include certain restrictions, known as *covenants*, which are certain other conditions or undertakings by the company which, if breached, may affect the terms of the security. Covenants are discussed further in Lesson 20.

RISK FACTORS

The risk factors section is a very important part of your investment analysis. Risks include negative factors or possible events that may negatively impact the company, such as losses, environmental liabilities, leverage, cash flow constraints, general economic conditions affecting the company, and regulatory issues.

Management discusses the risks and explains why the company feels the risks are reasonable or manageable—mitigants.

 Weighing Risks and Rewards   All companies face risks. It is important to determine whether the potential risks will impair the company's financial health and the value of the security, and whether the potential rewards from the security provide fair compensation for owning the security.

USING PROCEEDS FROM THE SALE

This section describes how the company intends to use the proceeds from the sale of the new securities. It's important to understand how the company intends to put your money to work. Why is the company issuing securities? Is the company building new plants? Is it buying new technology? Is it refinancing existing debt? Is it buying out the founders' common stock?

DESCRIPTION OF THE SECURITIES BEING OFFERED

This is the major part of the prospectus, and describes in detail the terms and conditions associated with the security being offered.

FINANCIAL STATEMENTS

The prospectus contains financial statements included in the annual report. It often contains pro forma information where the latest audit figures have been superseded, and a discussion of legal matters, the business, management, and other pertinent issues concerning the company.

 Keep an Open Mind Don't let these complex documents prevent you from choosing a particular investment. But make sure you understand the advantages and disadvantages of the security and the company before you invest.

In this lesson, you learned about the contents of a prospectus. In the next lesson, you learn about mutual fund prospectuses.

Mutual Fund Prospectuses

In this lesson, you learn about mutual fund prospectuses.

Description of the Fund

Like prospectuses associated with new security offerings, prospectuses for mutual funds explain the nature of the mutual fund and other relevant investment information.

Financial Highlights

The mutual fund prospectus lists highlights and summary data similar to the mutual fund annual report.

Investment Policies and Objectives

Mutual funds are managed to seek a variety of objectives from capital growth or appreciation, to current income, preservation of principal, and tax-advantaged income.

Investment Risk Investment risk is the uncertainty that an investment will yield a desired return or the possibility that a loss will occur.

RISK VERSUS REWARD

Mutual funds with the objective of preserving principal tend to invest in securities that bear relatively low risk, such as short-term money market instruments or U.S. Treasury securities. Mutual funds are designed to invest in securities that make current periodic interest payments and preserve principal.

On the other hand, growth-oriented mutual funds, which aim to achieve aggressive returns (income or growth), are prepared to assume greater risk to principal than income-type funds. Growth-oriented funds typically invest in common stocks. In between, mutual funds seeking growth tend to invest in common stocks. Mutual funds seeking current income tend to invest in fixed-income securities such as notes, bonds, and common stocks that pay regular dividends. Mutual funds seeking tax-advantaged income typically invest in notes and bonds issued by federal and municipal governments and government agencies that are exempt from federal and often state and local income taxes.

SERVICES

Other sections of the prospectus explain how to invest money in the mutual fund and how to redeem your mutual fund shares. You'll also find a description of the mutual fund's services and products.

In this lesson, you learned about the contents of mutual fund prospectuses. In the next lesson, you learn how to analyze companies by studying their financial statements.

7

QUALITATIVE COMPANY ANALYSIS

In this lesson, you learn how to use the qualitative information contained in annual reports as a basis for making sound investment decisions.

SLANTING INFORMATION

Annual reports and prospectuses are required to meet certain disclosure rules; however, there are a number of ways published information can be slanted in a company's favor without actually being false. For example, a company may minimize declining sales by writing that "the recession caused product sales to decline."

Your objective is to determine whether the information presented is accurate and reasonable. You then can apply your own intuition, experience, knowledge, and common sense to develop an overall investment strategy.

Look for outside sources that might confirm, contradict, or update the information found in an annual report. When discrepancies exist, investigate.

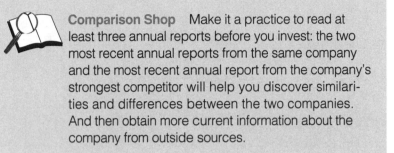

Comparison Shop   Make it a practice to read at least three annual reports before you invest: the two most recent annual reports from the same company and the most recent annual report from the company's strongest competitor will help you discover similarities and differences between the two companies. And then obtain more current information about the company from outside sources.

Look for inconsistencies in the information, including:

- This year's results better or worse than last year's
- Changes in top management
- Positives and negatives

FOLLOW THE MEDIA

Follow the business press and the media. News articles cover new developments about the economy, demographics, technological breakthroughs, laws and regulations, and industries and companies. General business magazines usually found in libraries include *Business Week, Forbes,* and *Fortune;* all provide analyses of companies.

You should also read *The Wall Street Journal* and other major business newspapers. Read current issues of personal finance magazines, including *Individual Investor, Kiplinger's Personal Finance, Money, Smart Money,* and *Worth.*

If you maintain an investment account with a full-service brokerage firm, take advantage of the firm's research capabilities and request financial analyst reports of companies that interest you.

THE INTERNET

If you have access to the Internet, you can search for information on industries and companies. The Internet enables you to obtain a vast array of investment information.

In this lesson, you learned about analyzing information in annual reports, and also about the kind of materials contained in annual reports. In the next lesson, you learn more about research and development and other information found in annual reports.

ANALYZING NEW PRODUCTS AND COMPETITORS

In this lesson, you learn about new products, competitors, and other factors affecting company business.

NEW PRODUCTS

A company's fortunes depend on its continuing capability to evolve with changing economics, technology, and demographics. This means developing and introducing new products and services. New products are particularly important in industries characterized by rapid change and heavy competition, and where patents play an important role. Such industries are pharmaceuticals, computers, electronics, and semiconductors.

RESEARCH AND DEVELOPMENT (R&D)

Research and development can lead to new products that increase sales, and new manufacturing processes, which, in turn, can lead to production efficiencies, lower production costs, and higher product quality.

 **R&D Expenditures**   You should expect technology and pharmaceutical companies to spend a significant amount of money on R&D. To some extent, companies in chemicals, consumer goods, and food will do the same.

! **Effective R&D Spending**   The effectiveness of R&D money spent—new products developed—is generally more important than the dollar amount of R&D spending.

COMPETITION

Often the most visible source of competition is other companies in the same industry. Most annual reports don't discuss specific competitors. Your objective should be to determine the nature and strength of the competition and how the company you are analyzing stacks up against the competition. Industry analyses cover competitive forces relevant to the industry.

THE ECONOMY

The U.S. economy has a relatively strong influence on a company's fortunes. The U.S. economy cycles up and down, and recessions typically occur every four years. Consumer spending and interest rates can have dramatic effects on companies' fortunes. The economics of foreign countries can also affect the U.S. companies. You as an investor must be conscious of these factors and how they impact the company you're considering investing in.

OUTSIDE EVENTS

Companies are affected by outside events. For example, when the weather is particularly poor, a theme park may experience poor attendance, which leads to lower sales and lower profits.

TRENDS

A *trend* is a pattern that moves in a particular direction over time. Two examples are the aging U.S. population and continuing reductions in the cost of technology. Look for trends that affect the company you are analyzing.

In this lesson, you learned how to evaluate a company based on product development and outside forces, including competition and the economy. In the next lesson, you learn more about analyzing companies through financial statements.

ANALYZING FINANCIAL STATEMENTS

In this lesson, you learn about analyzing companies through financial statements.

EXAMINING EQUIVALENT PERIODS

The key to making meaningful analyses of financial statements is to compare financial results for equivalent or comparable periods (like comparing "apples to apples"). This means comparing the third quarter of 1998 to the third quarter of 1997. When you compare equivalent periods, you can better assess the meaning of the financial information presented.

By analyzing the company's results of operations for two consecutive and equivalent periods at the same time, you can gain a sense of whether the company improved. Quarterly financial information can help you develop insight into how the company operates and how it makes its money.

When you review quarterly data, look for trends revealed in the numbers. Did this year's quarterly sales and profits increase over last year's? What percentage of total sales does each quarter represent? Did costs increase as a percentage of sales? Did the company generate more or less cash from its operations than the prior year or quarter?

IDENTIFYING INCONSISTENCIES

The causes of any changes between reporting periods may be important or immaterial, or they may be caused by a financial reporting inconsistency. Differences can signal underlying business problems or opportunities. Your objective is to determine the cause of the changes, the potential impact on the company, and the meaning of the changes from an investment standpoint. Does management's explanation of the changes make sense? Will the changes continue?

The 3%–5% Warning   Generally, a difference of more than 3%–5% from one period to the next, whether year to year or quarter to quarter, is considered to be material (significant) and warrants further analysis.

Even small changes in financial statement amounts may be important if they signify the beginning of a new trend. At the least, make a note of the difference for future reference.

INDUSTRY BENCHMARKS

Many industries have particular measurement systems and benchmarks that can be signs of a company's health.

In the retail industry, a measure of strength is same-store sales—the percentage increase in sales generated by stores that have been open for at least one year. This is a sign of the company's ability to sell more goods through its existing store base. Stores also measure their performance by sales dollars per square foot of retail selling (floor) space. In addition, chain stores often compare the results of one branch location against the results of other branches.

Measuring Yardsticks   Learn the yardsticks that are important to the company and its industry. Determine the yardstick's likely direction by reading articles and trade publications and financial analysts' reports. You can then form an opinion about the company's resulting financial position, and develop questions to get additional information you want to obtain to complete your analysis.

In this lesson, you learned more about analyzing financial statements. In the next lesson, you learn about the basic accounting principles.

Basic Accounting Principles

In this lesson, you learn about the accounting system that serves as the base for financial statements.

Bridging GAAP

The reporting system companies use to prepare financial statements is called GAAP, or Generally Accepted Accounting Principles. GAAP gives investors and financial analysts a common language to follow for interpreting and analyzing annual reports.

GAAP is a body of accounting and financial reporting rules and regulations that govern how financial activity and business transactions must be disclosed and presented in financial statements.

Governing Bodies

Accountants are responsible for the quality, accuracy, and consistency of the financial information presented in annual reports and prospectuses. Accountants see to it that company documents meet the minimum reporting and disclosure guidelines set forth by the Securities and Exchange Commission

(SEC), the Financial Accounting Standards Board (FASB), and certain committees of the American Institute of Certified Public Accountants (AICPA).

Financial statements found in the annual reports of publicly traded U.S. companies are prepared in accordance with GAAP. By law, independent auditors must study a company's financial statements and render an opinion as to whether the documents are in accordance with GAAP. If they aren't, the auditor's opinion will note inconsistencies or exceptions.

The following principles form the basis for GAAP.

REPORTING ENTITY OR ORGANIZATION

Companies present financial statements for a specific entity, such as the company as a whole or a group or individual subsidiary. The reporting entity is particularly important with respect to gaining an understanding of the business and the company you're investing in, the nature of the entity's obligations, and from where the company derives its cash flow.

MATERIALITY

Companies prepare financial statements that present the sum of *all* transactions and resulting balances from a period, grouped into like categories. In particular, the financial statements should fairly present those transactions that in total have *a material effect* on the company and the perception of the user of the financial statements.

SUBSTANCE VERSUS FORM

Financial statements attempt to present the substance of a company's business transactions. The legal form of the transaction is usually less important than the economic effect of the transaction on the company and its financial position.

REPORTING PERIODICITY

Reporting periodicity represents the period during which a company reports its financial results and financial position. The most common periods are the fiscal year and fiscal quarter. Periodicity helps companies organize financial information and helps users of financial statements compare financial data over equivalent periods of time. Quarterly financial information is particularly useful, especially for companies whose business is seasonal.

HISTORICAL COST

Business transactions and financial amounts are typically recorded at historical cost. This means the dollar amounts at which the assets were purchased or the liabilities were incurred.

Financial statements of U.S. companies and foreign companies that trade on a U.S. stock exchange are typically presented in U.S. dollars. The amounts are not adjusted for inflation. Sales earned from assets located in foreign countries are translated into U.S. dollars. Foreign currency translation is discussed in Lesson 24.

RESOURCES AND OBLIGATIONS

Financial statements, in particular the balance sheet, reflect a company's resources or assets, and its obligations or liabilities (concepts explained in later lessons).

PRINCIPLE OF CONSERVATISM

Accounting is based on the principle of conservatism. This means that sales revenue is recorded when it is earned, and expenses are recorded when it becomes known that they are likely to be incurred.

MATCHING PRINCIPLE

The goal of financial reporting is to summarize a company's financial activity during a given period of time. The matching principle reports financial activity and amounts that correspond to the company's business efforts during the relevant period. This concept of reflecting business activity in the financial statements regardless of when cash is received or paid is called accrual accounting and is explained in the next lesson.

In this lesson, you learned about the basic principles of accounting. In the next lesson, you learn about accrual accounting, which governs how financial statements are prepared.

11

ACCRUAL ACCOUNTING—NO CASH NOW

In this lesson, you learn about accrual accounting, which governs how financial statements are prepared.

ACCRUAL ACCOUNTING

Under accrual accounting, cash does not have to change hands for the company to recognize (record) a transaction. Instead, financial activity is recorded when a company earns revenue and when a capital transaction occurs.

 Accrual Method The accrual method of accounting means recording financial transactions in a company's books when the activity occurs—not necessarily when cash changes hands.

> **Cash Basis** Cash basis is an accounting method that recognizes revenues when cash is received and recognizes expenses when cash is paid out. Under cash basis accounting, a company can manage when it pays its bills and may have difficulty collecting cash, two events that can affect the company's reported earnings.

THE IMPORTANCE OF ACCRUAL ACCOUNTING

Accrual accounting is important because business activity is reported in the company's financial statements when sales revenue is earned and when expenses are incurred. The timing of recording and reporting transactions does not necessarily coincide with when the company collects or pays cash.

As you now know, publicly traded companies prepare their financial statements in accordance with GAAP, or Generally Accepted Accounting Principles. One of the main principles of GAAP is accrual accounting, which is based on the matching principle explained in Lesson 10. Under the matching principle, revenues and related expenses are matched together under accrual accounting.

REPORTING ACCRUED INTEREST EXPENSE

A common example of an accrued expense is interest on a loan. When a company borrows money, with the passage of time it owes the lender more interest. Even if payments are due in a future period, accrued interest expense represents the amount of interest expense owed as of the date of the financial statement. Recording the expense and obligation to pay interest helps to reflect more accurately the company's financial position since it owes the interest.

 Accrued Interest Expense Accrued interest is the amount of interest the company has incurred but not paid (owes) on its debt obligations—interest payable.

ASSETS WITH VALUE

Under accrual accounting, assets that have value and are expected to help the company generate sales and income in the future should be recorded on the company's balance sheet. Assets are written down when their value is less than the amount recorded on the balance sheet.

Write Down Write down means the company reduces the amount of an asset that is recorded on the balance sheet because the asset has declined in value. The write down is an expense item and reduces the company's income for the period.

In this lesson, you learned about concepts involved in accrual accounting. In the next lesson, you learn about the balance sheet.

THE BALANCE SHEET

In this lesson, you learn about the balance sheet and how to use the information it contains to make better investment decisions.

THE IMPORTANCE OF A BALANCE SHEET

The balance sheet is a financial statement that contains a company's resources (assets) and claims on those assets (liabilities and owners' equity). Balance sheets are designed to reflect a company's financial position as of a particular date, which is noted on the balance sheet.

Generally, balance sheets itemize material assets, liabilities, and owners' equity accounts as shown in Intel Corporation's balance sheet in Lesson 3.

 Remember this formula: Assets equal liabilities plus owners' equity.

ASSET CATEGORIES

Assets are resources of value that can provide future benefits to a company.

Assets vary depending on the nature of the company's business. For example, an electric utility owns generating stations that are significant fixed assets. Service businesses such as advertising agencies and accounting firms are likely to have fewer fixed assets.

Assets are divided into two general categories: current and noncurrent.

CURRENT ASSETS

Current assets are considered to be relatively liquid and are expected to be converted back into cash or used up within one year. Current assets are explained in Lesson 13.

NONCURRENT ASSETS

Noncurrent assets include property, plant, and equipment (PP&E) less accumulated depreciation, goodwill less accumulated amortization, other assets, and deferred charges. Noncurrent assets are resources that a company expects will provide economic benefits or value in the future.

LIABILITIES

Liabilities are the company's obligations to third parties. Like assets, liabilities are divided into two general categories: current and noncurrent.

CURRENT LIABILITIES

Current liabilities are due or expected to be paid within one year. Companies that have significant current liabilities and relatively low noncurrent liabilities may face a cash crunch. And a severe cash crunch can mean financial trouble. Current liabilities are explained in Lesson 19.

NONCURRENT LIABILITIES

Noncurrent liabilities are company obligations due or expected to be paid beyond one year. Noncurrent liabilities typically finance noncurrent assets such as PP&E.

OWNERS' EQUITY

Owners' equity is the difference between total assets and total liabilities. The formula Assets = Liabilities + Owners' Equity can be adjusted as follows: Assets – Liabilities = Owners' Equity.

Common stockholders "own" the company. The business owners or common stockholders bear the risk of first loss in the event the company is unable to pay off its creditors and preferred stockholders. But common stockholders benefit from the upside when a company succeeds.

Owners' equity represents the owners' claims on the company's assets after the liabilities have been satisfied, or the assets left over after liabilities have been paid.

Seeking Financial Strength   When you analyze a company, look for financial strength, which is often indicated by low debt and stable cash flow. Beware of companies with relatively high fixed costs and relatively poor or unstable cash flow.

FIXED-DEBT OBLIGATIONS

The first sign of financial strength or weakness is high leverage or borrowing. Companies capitalize themselves with debt, equity including preferred stock and common stock, and a number of other structured financial products. Because companies must continue to pay their debts—just like you must make your mortgage and car payments—regardless of the level of sales revenue, debt represents a fixed cost.

!

50 Percent Threshold   Beware of companies whose debt-to-total capital ratio exceeds 50 percent. It is important to determine whether these companies can meet their debt obligations, especially during a recession.

When a company's leverage exceeds 50 percent, this does not necessarily mean a company is in financial trouble, especially if the company can generate enough cash from operations to cover its obligations. Generally, though, the less debt and other fixed obligations a company takes on, the more financial flexibility it retains.

MATCHING ASSETS AND LIABILITIES

Another signal of financial strength is the way a company finances its assets and operations. Accounts payable, which is a current liability, finances the purchase of inventory, which is a current asset. Debt and equity finance the remaining assets.

It is often a sign of financial stability when a company has long-term debt to finance its long-term assets, and short-term debt to finance its current assets. This is called match-funding assets and liabilities.

 Review the debt footnote to determine the structure and terms and conditions of the company's debt and lease obligations.

In this lesson, you learned about the components of a balance sheet that help you analyze a company. In the next lesson, you learn about current assets.

13

CURRENT ASSETS

In this lesson, you learn about the nature of current assets, including cash and marketable securities, accounts receivable, inventories, prepaid expenses, non-trade receivables, and restricted cash.

LIQUID RESOURCES—NEARLY CASH

Current assets are company-owned or -controlled resources that will be consumed or used up within the next year or current operating cycle. Current assets can also be viewed as operating resources. In other words, a company uses current assets in the day-to-day operation of its business. Current assets are presented in the balance sheet from top to bottom with the assets closest to cash—most liquid—appearing at the top.

CASH AND MARKETABLE SECURITIES

Cash generally includes money held in checking and demand deposit accounts; petty cash; and operating cash, which is particularly common to retailers.

Marketable securities include short-term investments that the company made with excess cash. Generally, these securities include short-term money market instruments and overnight deposits with financial institutions.

Excessive cash balances often lower a company's overall rate of return on equity.

ACCOUNTS RECEIVABLE

Accounts receivable means a company is "owed" money. When a customer buys a product today, the company prepares an invoice (bill), which typically gives the buyer 30 days to pay in full. Accounts receivable is perhaps the most important current asset and is discussed in more detail in Lesson 14.

INVENTORY

Inventory represents goods held for sale by a company. Inventory is discussed in further detail in Lesson 15.

NON-TRADE RECEIVABLES

Non-trade receivables represent monies due the company from sources other than customer purchases. Non-trade receivables include tax refunds receivable, investment income receivable, and amounts owed the company from the sale of PP&E.

RESTRICTED CASH

Restricted cash is earmarked for a specific purpose usually in accordance with a legal document or contract. A company cannot use restricted cash freely to fund its business operations, so restricted cash must be segregated from the "cash and marketable securities" balance. Restricted cash is shown separately on the balance sheet or included in other assets.

PREPAID ASSETS

Prepaid assets are current assets where the company has paid the bill in advance of receiving the service or benefit or where the company will receive benefits during the next year or operating cycle. An example of this is insurance coverage.

The Current ratio and Quick ratio measure a company's short-term liquidity strength.

Current ratio measures a company's capability to use its current assets to pay off its current liabilities. It is calculated as current assets divided by current liabilities.

> **Liquidity Power**   Generally, a current ratio of 2:1 or more is considered to be reasonable. Generally, the higher the ratio, the stronger the financial strength of the company, but ratios are relative and depend on the company and the industry.

READING THE CURRENT RATIO

The more stable the company and the industry, the more likely the company is to generate relatively stable and predictable cash flow, so a Current ratio of less than 2:1 might be acceptable. For unstable companies and industries such as fad or high-risk research and development-related companies and industries, the higher the Current ratio, the better. This is because high current assets means the company has a relatively high amount of liquid assets to fund its operations.

Follow the trend in a company's Current ratio. An unusually large change from one period to the next may indicate a temporary blip in the company's financial position, or perhaps a new trend.

QUICK RATIO

The Quick ratio also measures a company's capability to pay its short-term liabilities. While the Current ratio compares total current assets to total current liabilities, the Quick ratio pays particular attention to the liquidity of current assets; inventory is excluded from current assets used in the Quick ratio.

The Quick ratio equals the sum of cash, marketable securities, and accounts receivable divided by current liabilities.

 One to One   Look for a Quick ratio of at least 1:1 or higher. A ratio of 1:1 means the company has enough relatively liquid assets to pay its current liabilities.

Ratio Analysis   Ratios are useful to help you analyze a company and its financial position. However, it is important to compare ratios of the same company and to other companies within the same industry for equivalent periods and over successive years. Look to see whether the ratios are improving or deteriorating.

Looking at a company's liquidity strength another way, consider working capital.

Working Capital   Working capital is the amount of the company's net investment in its operating cycle—the net amount the company can use to fund its operations:

Working Capital = Current Assets – Current Liabilities

Higher working capital may mean the company has more short-term liquidity to meet its short-term liabilities.

In this lesson, you learned about how to measure and interpret current assets. In the next lesson, you learn about accounts receivable.

14

ACCOUNTS RECEIVABLE— YOU OWE ME

In this lesson, you learn how to analyze accounts receivable.

CUSTOMER'S IOUs

Accounts receivable represent money customers owe a company for goods or services purchased. When a company sells goods and services on account—that is to say, extends credit to its customers—the company records those transactions as accounts receivable.

Accounts receivable is a current asset on the company's balance sheet because the company expects to collect cash from its customers to pay cash within one year or sooner.

MAINTAINING SCHEDULES

Companies maintain schedules of their accounts receivable and track each account by its scheduled payment date or due date.

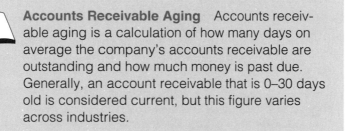

Accounts Receivable Aging   Accounts receivable aging is a calculation of how many days on average the company's accounts receivable are outstanding and how much money is past due. Generally, an account receivable that is 0–30 days old is considered current, but this figure varies across industries.

Accounts receivable that are outstanding for more than 30 days are typically considered past due. The notion of "past due" depends on the credit terms the company offers and industry custom. The older the accounts receivable, the less likely a company will collect its money.

Accounts Receivable Turnover   Accounts receivable turnover is the number of times a company collects its accounts receivable during the year.

An effective way to analyze a company's capability to collect its receivables is to compute accounts receivable turnover. Accounts receivable turnover equals sales on credit divided by average accounts receivable.

The higher a company's accounts receivable turnover ratio, the more efficiently the company is collecting its accounts receivable and converting credit sales into cash.

FAST CASH

Because companies need cash to fund their operations, the faster a company collects its accounts receivable, the more quickly and efficiently it can reinvest the cash in the business. Beware when the average collection period increases significantly year to year.

Average Collection Period   Average collection period is the average number of days a company takes to collect its accounts receivable.

Average collection period equals accounts receivable turnover ratio divided by 360 days.

The higher a company's accounts receivable turnover and the shorter its average collection period, the more profitable the company should be. In effect, the sooner a company converts its accounts receivable into cash, the less borrowings the company should need to run its operations.

Allowance for Doubtful Accounts   Allowance for doubtful accounts is that portion (percentage) of accounts receivable the company does not expect to collect. This balance sheet account is shown as a reduction of accounts receivable.

In practice, it is rare for a company to collect 100 percent of its accounts receivable. Write-offs arise because a certain percentage of a company's customers don't pay their bills, or some customers may declare bankruptcy.

Based on the company's experience with past write-offs, it recognizes an allowance for doubtful accounts. The company writes off or expenses a percentage of its accounts receivable each period.

Bad Debt Expense   Bad debt expense is the company's estimate of the accounts receivable it will not collect.

Beware when the allowance for doubtful accounts as a percent of accounts receivable increases significantly. This can be a sign of lax credit policies and more write-offs.

In this lesson, you learned how accounts receivable relates to a company's financial health. In the next lesson, you learn about inventory.

15

INVENTORY—
GOODS FOR SALE

In this lesson, you learn about inventory and its importance to a company's manufacturing and selling efforts.

GOODS

Inventory represents the goods a company offers for sale and the materials a company uses to produce those goods. Inventory is a current asset and is generally used up or converted into cash within one year.

GOODS FOR SALE

Many retailers purchase the goods they offer for sale—finished goods from other companies, known as suppliers or vendors.

Manufacturers typically maintain three types of inventory: raw materials, work-in-process (WIP), and finished goods.

The three inventory sub-accounts—raw materials, work-in-process, and finished goods—are typically added together and presented as one inventory amount on a company's balance sheet. Sometimes the company provides additional information about its inventory in footnotes.

RAW MATERIALS INVENTORY

Manufacturers typically purchase raw materials—the basic ingredients of the products they produce. Of the three inventory categories, raw materials may be the easiest to dispose of for cash, since it is relatively generic. Manufacturers move raw materials into production (WIP).

WORK-IN-PROCESS

As its name implies, work-in-process inventory includes items currently in the company's manufacturing process. Work-in-process inventory includes the cost of the materials put into production plus direct manufacturing costs.

Direct manufacturing costs include direct labor and factory overhead. Direct labor includes wages and benefits for factory workers. Factory overhead includes the cost of operating plants and manufacturing facilities. After the goods are completed, the company transfers the work-in-process inventory into finished goods inventory.

FINISHED GOODS INVENTORY

Finished goods inventory is completed goods the company offers for sale. Eventually inventory is either sold or scrapped, at which time the cost of finished goods inventory is charged through the income statement as an expense—cost of goods sold. Under the best circumstances, customers purchase all of the company's finished goods inventory at full price and there are no returns.

> Beware of rising inventory. Most companies need a certain amount of inventory on hand to meet sales, but inventory also ties up capital. When a company's inventory balloons and its market changes, losses are usually not far behind.

When companies launch new products and open new sites, they generally increase their inventory. Increasing sales often are accompanied by increasing inventory, and more inventory is often necessary to support an expanding sales base.

> Beware of economic cycles and their effect on the company's raw materials prices, their profit margins, and cash flow. When companies purchase raw materials, their inventory costs often rise during times of economic prosperity when there is expansion and fall during recessions. This affects profit margins.

LIFO AND FIFO

Companies follow two general methods of inventory accounting:

- First-In-First-Out (FIFO)
- Last-In-First-Out (LIFO)

These methods describe how the cost of inventory flows through the income statement as cost of goods sold (COGS).

The cost flow for accounting purposes does not necessarily mirror the physical flow of the goods.

Under FIFO, the cost of the oldest inventory is charged to COGS first. Under LIFO, the cost of the newest inventory is charged to COGS first. In times of falling prices, FIFO increases COGS and reduces profits. In times of rising prices, LIFO increases COGS and reduces profits.

ACCOUNTING FOR INVENTORY

Inventory should be capitalized on a company's balance sheet at the lower of historical cost and market value. Historical cost is the cost at which the company purchased the inventory. The cost of inventory should include all costs associated with getting the inventory ready for sale, including shipping the inventory to the company's warehouse and manufacturing the inventory. The cost of inventory should be reduced for any discounts given by the vendors.

Lower of cost and market means the company records inventory at historical cost but writes it down—expenses it—when it becomes aware of a decline in the inventory's market value.

INVENTORY TURNOVER

Inventory turnover measures a company's capability to sell its inventory and process its inventory through its production system. Inventory turnover equals the cost of goods sold divided by average inventory.

Seeking High Inventory Turnover   The better a company sells its products and manages its investment in inventory, and the more efficiently it produces goods, the higher the inventory turnover is. The more times a company can "sell its inventory," the less capital the company needs to finance its inventory and the lower its interest expense.

You should analyze the inventory turnover in conjunction with accounts receivable. To increase sales, companies may sell their goods to companies with poor credit ratings. Financially weak customers often pay their bills late or never pay them at all. This can lead to losses for the seller.

Compare inventory turnover ratios of two companies in the same industry group. Inventory turnover differs across companies and industries and ratios may be different based on seasonality.

Deteriorating Inventory Turnover   Beware of slower, weak, and deteriorating inventory turnover and increases in inventory in the absence of sales increases.

In this lesson, you learned about inventory and inventory turnover. In the next lesson, you learn about fixed assets including property, plant, and equipment.

PROPERTY, PLANT, AND EQUIPMENT

In this lesson, you learn about property, plant, and equipment.

MAKING THE PRODUCTS

Property, plant, and equipment (PP&E) are long-term or non-current assets owned or controlled by a company and used to manufacture and/or sell the company's products. The balance sheet typically shows all categories of PP&E grouped together, net of accumulated depreciation. PP&E helps you determine the nature of the company's business and its need for long-term financing.

Depreciation Depreciation is the write-off or expensing of a percentage of the historical cost of an asset over the asset's useful life.

Depreciation represents wear and tear on an asset or the fact that an asset gets used up over time. Companies record depreciation expense in the income statement every year for all depreciable assets in service or used by the company during the year.

Accumulated Depreciation   Accumulated depreciation is the total or cumulative depreciation expense the company records for all its assets in service.

TYPES OF DEPRECIATION

There are two general categories of depreciation:

- **Straight-line**   Under straight-line depreciation, the asset's historical cost is written off in equal amounts during each year of the asset's estimated useful life.

- **Accelerated**   Under accelerated expenses, a larger percentage of an asset's historical cost is written off during the early years of an asset's useful life and a smaller percentage is written off during the later years. There are two types of accelerated depreciation: sum-of-the-years'-digits and double declining balance.

Under different depreciation methods, the annual depreciation expense may differ, but the total depreciation for an asset will be the same over the asset's useful life.

The footnotes to the financial statements generally list PP&E by category, and total PP&E is carried forward and listed on the balance sheet under PP&E. The balance sheet shows PP&E net of accumulated depreciation.

Net Book Value   Net book value equals the assets' historical cost minus accumulated depreciation.

Dueling Systems—Tax versus Accounting

Income tax depreciation often differs from accounting or book depreciation. The Internal Revenue Service allows companies to depreciate certain assets under accelerated depreciation. Most profitable companies record accelerated depreciation for income tax purposes and straight-line depreciation for accounting purposes. By using accelerated depreciation for income taxes, companies can reduce the amount of income taxes they have to pay the IRS. And, by using straight-line depreciation for GAAP financial statements instead of accelerated depreciation, companies can increase their GAAP earnings.

The difference between GAAP and Tax Accounting methods is handled through deferred taxes, which is discussed in Lesson 28.

Land is not depreciable because it is considered to last forever.

 Buildings Buildings include real estate and other real property that is permanently attached to the ground.

Real estate companies that buy and sell properties are likely to account for their real estate as inventory. If the company owns its headquarters, it would account for this property as a fixed asset and not as inventory.

The Significant Accounting Policies footnote generally describes the depreciation methods a company uses and the number of years over which it depreciates its PP&E.

DIFFERING METHODS

Different companies in the same industry may depreciate their assets over different useful lives and under different depreciation methods. This can make it difficult for you to make a meaningful comparison of companies.

Land that is mined for natural resources, such as gold or oil, is subject to depletion, the expensing of a natural resource asset based on mining activity.

Depletion   For companies that mine natural resources, depletion is the accounting method that reduces the value of real property as its resources are depleted with a subsequent reduction in taxable income.

Companies record depletion expense based on the actual usage such as tons mined. They calculate depletion per unit based on the cost of the mine, for example, and the estimated amount of natural resources. *Accumulated depletion* is similar to accumulated depreciation.

LEASING EQUIPMENT

Companies lease assets from third parties in order to maintain flexibility over their PP&E and preserve capital. There are two categories of leases: operating leases and capital leases.

Leased Assets   Leased assets are assets where the company has the right to use the asset for a portion of or substantially all of the leased asset's economic useful life.

Operating leases are normally short-term leases where the lessee, or equipment user, uses the asset for only a portion of the asset's useful economic life. Operating leases are discussed further in Lesson 21.

Operating leases are normally short-term leases where the lessee, or equipment user, uses less than 90 percent of the asset's useful economic life. Assets under operating leases are not recorded on the company's balance sheet. Instead, the company's rent obligation is disclosed in the lease commitment footnote.

Assets under capital lease represent a purchase of the asset by the company because the company controls the asset for substantially all of the entire useful life of the asset. Assets under capital lease are also included in PP&E.

A capital lease is accounted for as a leasehold asset, and a corresponding liability is called a leasehold obligation. The leasehold obligation equals the present value of the minimum lease payments due under the capital lease—the rent payments reduced by the interest component. This leasehold obligation is considered to be a debt obligation of the company.

 Amortizing Leases   Assets under capital lease are written off (amortized) over the shorter of the lease term and the asset's economic useful life.

Capital lease payments are split between principal and interest payments. Capital leases are considered that the lessee owns the leased asset for accounting purposes and treats the lease rental payments as debt—principal and interest.

Leasehold Improvements   Improvements or enhancements made to property under lease. Leasehold improvements are written off over the shorter of the improvement's economic useful life and the remainder of the lease term.

In this lesson, you learned about long-term fixed assets, including PP&E and depreciation. In the next lesson, you learn about other long-term assets.

OTHER LONG-TERM ASSETS

In this lesson, you learn about more long-term assets, including intangible assets.

INTANGIBLE ASSETS

Intangible assets are assets that have value to a company, although you can't touch or see them. Intangible assets include organization costs, patents and copyrights, trademarks, trade names, and goodwill.

Goodwill arises when one company acquires another company and pays a premium over the target company's owners equity. In effect, goodwill is the premium the acquirer pays for the target company's established business, over and above the cost of its infrastructure.

AMORTIZATION

Amortization is the write-off or expensing of the cost of a financial instrument or an intangible asset over the shorter of its useful or legal life. Amortization is similar to depreciation and reflects the declining useful life and value of the intangible asset over time.

Generally, intangible assets are amortized over the shorter of the asset's legal life and its estimated useful life. Under GAAP, intangible assets should be amortized over at least five years and not more than 40 years. Intangible assets do not include PP&E.

Companies in research and development (R&D) intensive fields typically have many patents. Such industries include high technology (computers, electronics), pharmaceuticals, and chemicals. Companies that invent new products and processes file patents to protect their invention and prevent other companies from using their invention.

Companies also preserve their rights to written works (books, manuals, etc.) through copyrights and protect their company and brand names by registering their trademarks.

Other assets also include PP&E that are not currently in service that are held for disposal or sale, and long-term assets that don't meet the other asset categories. Other assets can include research and development costs. However, most research and development expenditures (R&D) are expensed in the year they are incurred.

In this lesson, you learned about intangible assets, including patents and copyrights. In the next lesson, you learn about investments.

Investments— Earning Income on Extra Cash

In this lesson, you learn about investments. Companies invest money to earn interest income on idle cash and to enter other businesses.

Investing for Income

Investment is the purchase of securities and other financial instruments to earn financial income. Investments range from short-term cash instruments to more risky growth vehicles.

 Short-Term Investments Short-term investments include interest-bearing securities or deposits that mature in less than one year.

Short-term investments are typically liquid, which means they can be converted into cash relatively easily. Short-term investments are recorded in the cash/cash equivalents balance in the current asset section of the balance sheet.

Accounting for Financial Investments

Companies record their investments in the following categories: Held to maturity, Trading, and Available for sale.

Investments held to maturity means the company intends to hold such securities, usually bonds, to maturity. Investments held to maturity are recorded on the balance sheet at amortized cost.

Trading investments are investments the company expects to trade—sell—in a short period of time. Trading investments are recorded on the balance sheet at estimated fair market value. Unrealized gains and losses are reflected in the results of continuing operations.

Investments available for sale are investments the company may sell depending on market prices, investment outlook, and the company's cash needs. Investments available for sale are recorded on the balance sheet at estimated fair market value, with unrealized gains and losses reflected as a separate component of shareholder's equity, net of taxes.

Long-Term Investments   Long-term investments can include shares of common stock of another company, the company intends to hold for more than one year.

Accounting for Equity Investments

There are three accounting methods for investments: Cost method (less than 20 percent ownership), Equity method (between 20–50 percent ownership), and Consolidated subsidiary method (at least 50 percent ownership).

The accounting method depends on the percentage of the company the investor owns and the degree of influence and control the company can exercise over the investment.

COST METHOD

For investments accounted for under the cost method, the investments are recorded on the balance sheet at the investment's purchase price and are adjusted for downward changes in market value. When the investor receives dividend payments, the investor records the dividends as dividend income.

EQUITY METHOD

For investments accounted for under the equity method, the investor records the initial investment on the gross balance sheet at the cost of the investment and adjusts the investment balance to recognize its share of earnings from the investment less dividends.

> **!** **Footnoting Methodology** The company's accounting methodology should be described in the significant account policies footnote. Beware of changes in the classification of investments, which can alter earnings.

OWNING SUBSIDIARIES

Subsidiaries are investments in companies when the investing company—the owner/investor—usually owns at least 50 percent of the investment or when the investor can exert significant influence or control over the investment.

In this lesson, you learned about investments and several ways to account for investments. In the next lesson, you learn about current liabilities.

CURRENT LIABILITIES

In this lesson, you learn about current liabilities, including accounts payable, short-term borrowing, and current portion of long-term debt.

IOU SOON

Current liabilities are IOUs or obligations of the company to be paid within one year. Current liabilities are obligations that arise from the purchase of current assets and the portion of a long-term liability that becomes due within one year.

BUYING INVENTORY AND INCREASING ACCOUNTS PAYABLE

Accounts payable are amounts owed to the company's suppliers for the purchase of inventory. Companies typically buy inventory on credit; and the bill may be due in 30 days for example. Accounts payable is a very common form of short-term financing. Accounts payable is often called supplier financing.

> ! Beware of increasing accounts payable, especially in the absence of increasing sales and in the presence of declining cash flow. In effect, the higher a company's current liabilities, the weaker its current ratio.

Short-Term Borrowing   Short-term borrowing includes notes and loans owed to third parties payable within one year.

BORROWING MONEY

Short term loans are due within one year and a portion of long-term debt is due in the current year. These are accounted for as current liabilities. Over time, long-term liabilities typically become current liabilities. Accrued interest expense is interest owed but not paid.

Long-Term Debt   Long-term debt includes company obligations due beyond one year, such as a 10-year note. Long-term debt is a noncurrent liability, although the installments due within one year are accounted for as current liabilities.

Long-Term Debt-Current Portion   Long-term debt-current portion means payments of long-term debt due within one year.

Accrued Wages   Accrued wages means the amount of salary and wages expense owed to employees.

Unearned Revenue   Unearned revenue means advance deposits the company collects from its customers, but when the company has not completed its duties to finalize the earnings process.

An example of unearned revenue are insurance premiums collected at the beginning of the year for the upcoming year.

OTHER PAYABLES

Other payables include other short-term obligations the company expects to pay within one year.

Examples of other payables include taxes payable, and other liabilities arising out of lawsuits or other claims against the company.

In this lesson, you learned about the different types of current liabilities. In the next lesson, you learn about long-term liabilities.

NONCURRENT LIABILITIES

In this lesson, you learn about noncurrent liabilities.

NONCURRENT IOUs

Noncurrent liabilities are company obligations to be paid beyond one year. The major components of long-term liabilities include long-term debt, long-term notes and bonds payable, mortgages payable, capital lease obligations, pension liability, and deferred tax liability.

 Principal of Long-Term Debt   Principal means the balance of the debt owed. Generally, this equals the amount of money borrowed, less principal installments paid to date.

Bonds payable is recorded on the company's balance sheet as the amount of money owed today. This is called the outstanding amount of the obligation. Long-term debt excludes interest payable on the debt because interest accrues with the passage of time.

Terms and Conditions   Debt is subject to terms, conditions, and covenants including interest rate, maturity date, required payments, and collateral. These are generally described in the debt footnote.

BREACHING COVENANTS

Covenants are qualitative and quantitative requirements and restrictions placed on the company. A covenant may include a debt-to-total capital ratio of less than 50 percent. When a company breaches a covenant it is in default on its obligations, and if the company doesn't cure or clear the default within a certain agreed-on time frame—the grace or cure period—the lenders can call the long-term debt.

Calling Debt   Calling debt means requiring immediate repayment in full.

MANAGING DEBT

Most loan agreements and bond indentures require the borrower to make periodic debt service payments of principal and interest during the life of the loan. These payments amortize the loan.

Amortization   Amortization of a debt instrument is the extinguishment or paying down of the obligation over time through periodic payments of principal and interest.

An example of amortization is a home mortgage where the homeowner or borrower makes monthly payments of principal and interest.

> ! **Big IOUs**   Beware of large amounts of debt coming due to a company within the next few years.

Does the company have the cash flow to repay the debt? Or can the company refinance the debt?

 Face Value or Par Value   Face value or par value is the principal amount of the debt or the amount owed. For bonds, face value is $1,000.

When a company sells or issues a bond at par, the investor or lender pays the face value of $1,000. The company collects the proceeds from the issuance of the bonds minus the financial institution's arrangement or underwriting fee.

 Stated Interest Rate or Coupon Rate   Stated interest rate or coupon rate is the interest rate the company promises to pay.

The issuance price of a bond is set based on the market interest rates on the day the bond is issued compared to the bond's stated interest rate or coupon. Bonds are issued at a premium or discount where the bonds' stated interest rate differs from the current market interest rates.

Premium Premium is the excess proceeds from the issuance of a bond, where the coupon payment exceeds the current market interest rate.

When a bond's coupon rate is higher than the current market interest rate—for example, 10 percent versus a market interest rate of 9 percent—investors will pay a premium for that bond because investors earn the market yield. The investors and the company would amortize the premium over the life of the bond.

Discount Discount is the difference between the proceeds from the issuance of a bond and the face value, where the coupon payment is less than the current market interest rate.

Debt and Leverage Generally, lower debt or lower leverage gives a company more financial and operating flexibility than companies with higher debt and higher leverage. Beware of debt-to-total capital ratios that exceed 50 percent.

In this lesson, you learned about long-term borrowings. In the next lesson, you learn about footnotes to financial statements.

INFORMATION CONTAINED IN FOOTNOTES

In this lesson, you learn how to read footnotes to financial statements.

THE GOLD MINE OF INFORMATION

Footnotes are explanatory text that accompany financial statements and are designed to clarify the numbers shown in financial statements. Study the footnotes to financial statements closely because they can reveal important information about the company and its financial position.

SIGNIFICANT ACCOUNTING POLICIES

Note 1 describes the significant accounting policies—the methods a company uses to prepare its financial statements. Significant accounting policies include revenue recognition, accounting for depreciation, inventory, investments, and fixed assets. Note that the permitted accounting methods should be in conformity with GAAP, or the auditor's opinion should note the exception.

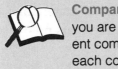

Comparing Footnotes   Read the footnotes when you are analyzing the financial statements of different companies in the same industry. Make sure each company uses the same or consistent accounting methods from year to year. If the accounting methods differ, assess the impact of the differences on each company's financial position.

CHANGING ACCOUNTING SYSTEMS

When a company changes its accounting methods and there is a material difference between the financial statements with and without the change, the company restates all financial statements shown. The goal of financial reporting is to show financial results that are consistent from year to year—apples to apples. The independent auditor's opinion should explain material changes in accounting methods.

Other footnotes include commitments and contingent liabilities, financial instruments, taxes, pensions, investments, acquisitions and divestitures, borrowings, income taxes, transactions involving the company's common stock, litigation, environmental liability and exposure, and subsequent events.

If applicable, a "subsequent events" note will describe significant events that occured between the end of the company's fiscal year and the date the company issued its annual report.

Subsequent Events   Subsequent events disclosed are expected to have a material effect on the company's financial position.

Footnotes may include some or all of the items mentioned above, depending on the company's business, the materiality of an event, and the company's activities for the years presented in the financial statements.

> **Financial Instruments**   Financial instruments include derivatives and other financial contracts.

Hedging Transactions

Companies can use financial instruments to hedge their assets and liabilities or to speculate. One example of a hedging transaction is a company protecting its overseas sales and income from fluctuating exchange rates between a local currency such as Japanese yen and U.S. dollars.

Companies also use derivatives to hedge their interest rate exposure. Some companies have also used derivatives and other financial instruments for speculation, which tends to carry significantly more risk than hedging transactions.

Making Commitments

Two major commitments are:

- Obligations to pay rent under a lease
- Future purchases of goods and services

> **Commitments**   Commitments include obligations that are not included in the financial statements and have not fallen due but will contractually fall due at some point in the future.

Financial statements reflect the sum of all financial transactions, and resulting balances from a period are grouped into like categories. Commitments are typically disclosed in the footnotes. You must determine whether any commitments and contingencies disclosed in the footnotes will have a negative effect on the company when they contractually fall due.

Capital Leases and Operating Leases

Leases are a common form of financing, where an owner buys an asset and leases the asset of the company (lessee). You may have leased a car or rented an apartment.

> **Operating Leases**   Operating leases are agreements where the company (lessee) agrees to use (rent) the asset for a portion of the asset's useful life. At the end of the lease term, the company normally returns the asset to the lessor and walks away.

Operating leases differ from capital leases (which were discussed in Lesson 16) in that the term of operating leases extends for a portion of the asset's economic useful life (less than 90 percent). Under an operating lease, the risks and rewards associated with ownership of the leased property typically reside with the lessor.

The footnote also would separately list any rent the company expects to earn on subleases when the company rents out part or all of a property to a third party.

Operating lease commitments are not shown in the company's balance sheet. Rather, they are shown in the lease commitment footnote. Operating lease (rent) payments are recorded as rent expense when they are made.

The lease commitment footnote also includes a description of any other significant information regarding the company's leasing activity. This may include residual value guarantees and extra rent due based on sales volume or actual usage level of the asset—known as contingent rent.

Contingencies   Contingencies are liabilities that may arise depending on the outcome of certain events.

Companies evaluate contingencies based on the likelihood events will occur and whether the future outcome of current events may generate income or expenses. Remote, unlikely events are typically not disclosed. If a contingency may possibly occur, management should disclose the information in the footnotes. Also, if the contingency is probable to occur, management must estimate the loss and record an accrued liability and expense in the financial statements.

Litigation   Litigation means legal proceedings, actions, and lawsuits in which other parties are seeking enforcement against the company; actions the company is pursuing against other parties. Litigation exposure is usually in the form of contingency liability.

Here are some common litigation actions:

- Shareholder class actions
- Infringement of patents, trademarks, copyrights, and other intellectual property rights
- Product liability claims caused by defective products
- Personal injury cases
- Environmental damage to property resulting in cleanup
- Violation of laws
- Employee actions involving cases of wrongful dismissal, discrimination, etc.
- Insurance claims

In this lesson, you learned about what information is included in footnotes. In the next lesson, you learn about pensions.

Pensions and Retirement Benefits

In this lesson, you learn about pensions and pension benefits.

Income for Staying Home

If you work for a company that provides you with a pension, you're already familiar with how pension plans work. Pensions can be a particularly significant obligation for a company, especially when the company employs unionized workers. Annual reports include information about company pension plans in the footnotes.

Payments for Life

Pensions are a company's promise to pay retirement benefits to employees. There are two types of pension plans:

- Defined contribution plans
- Defined benefit plans

Defined contribution plans are retirement plans in which the company contributes a fixed amount of money to the plan today and offers participating employees several general investment options. The amount of the employee's pensions ultimately depends on the actual performance of the investments. When a participating employee retires, he or she can make withdrawals from the plan equal to the value of his or her investments.

The two most common defined contribution plans are 401(k) and 403(b) plans. Employees can elect to make contributions directly from their salaries through payroll deductions. Often the company matches a percentage of the employee's contributions.

Under defined contribution plans, once the company funds its obligation today, the company has no additional obligation to provide additional pension benefits.

Defined benefit plans are pension plans where the company or the plan promises to pay retired employees a certain amount of money (benefits) every year beginning when the employee retires. Defined benefit plans generally begin paying benefits when the former employer reaches age 62 or 65 and continue for the remainder of the employee's life.

For the company to meet its pension obligations under a defined benefit plan, the company has to contribute money to the plan today and invest the money such that it will grow to meet the contractual or defined benefits.

Pension plan assets are generally held by a trust or investment company, so they are *not* carried on the company's balance sheet. The company's pension liability is the shortfall between the present value of the plan's obligations to pay benefits and the actual value of the plan's investments and is explained in the pension footnote.

Future pension obligations are based on assumptions about investment returns of the pension portfolio, years of employee service (number of years the employee works), employee life expectancy, employee salary (which is the basis for pension benefit calculation), and vesting period.

Vesting Period   Vesting period is the number of years the company requires a worker to be an employee of the company for the employee to be eligible to collect benefits. Full vesting generally occurs at five years, although some employees may be partially vested before then.

Recognizing Expense   Under defined benefit pension plans, companies recognize expense during each year the employee works. This follows the matching principle.

CHANGING SITUATIONS

As the pension assumptions change, a company's pension liability and expense will change. An example is investment returns compared to expected returns. If the actual return is less than the expected return, the company would owe money to the pension plan and the pension plan assets would not grow enough to meet the money needed to pay the benefits.

Because the pension plan footnote and related calculations are complex, you should look primarily at these two points:

* Reasonableness of the projected rate of return

* Fair market value of pension plan assets compared to pension plan benefit obligation

Beware of a pension plan that is significantly underfunded. When actual investment returns are less than expected returns, the pension plan may have too few assets to pay the retirees. Then the company will owe more money to the pension plan to make up the shortfall.

As an employee, you should be concerned about the health of your company's pension plan because you are counting on this money for your retirement income. As an investor, you should be concerned about a significant shortfall in the pension plan assets and the cost to the company of contributing additional assets to the plan.

Post-retirement employee health benefits are also treated in a similar fashion as pensions. Companies are required to record these expenses during the employee's working life. This expense estimate equals the amount of money the company expects to pay for those employees' health benefits during retirement.

In this lesson, you learned about pensions and the pension footnote. In the next lesson, you learn about the independent auditor's opinion.

THE AUDITOR'S OPINION

23

In this lesson, you learn about the independent auditor's opinion.

ENDORSING THE FINANCIAL STATEMENTS

An auditor's opinion is the company's independent auditor's endorsement of the fairness of the financial statements and whether the financial statements are presented in accordance with GAAP.

Fulfilling GAAP The audit is an in-depth method for confirming the accuracy and reasonableness of the financial statements in relation to GAAP. However, the audit only gives users of financial statements comfort that the financial statements present fairly the company's financial position as of the date of the report in accordance with GAAP.

To the Board of Directors and Shareholders:

We have audited the accompanying consolidated balance sheets of the Company and subsidiaries as of December 31, 1998 and 1997, and the related consolidated statements of income, shareholders' equity, and cash flows for each of the two years ended December 31, 1998 and 1997. These financial statements are the responsibility of the Company's management. Our responsibility is to express an opinion on these financial statements based on our audits.

We conducted our audits in accordance with generally accepted auditing standards. Those standards require that we plan and perform the audit to obtain reasonable assurance about whether the financial statements are free of material misstatement. An audit includes examining, on a test basis, evidence supporting the amounts and disclosures in the financial statements. An audit also includes assessing the accounting principles used and significant estimates made by management, as well as evaluating the overall financial statement presentation. We believe that our audits provide a reasonable basis for our opinion.

In our opinion, the financial statements referred to above present fairly, in all material respects, the consolidated financial position of the Company and subsidiaries at December 31, 1998 and 1997, and the consolidated results of its operations and its cash flows for each of the two years in the period ended December 31, 1998, in conformity with generally accepted accounting principles (GAAP).

Independent Audit Firm

New York, New York

January 31, 1999

GARDEN VARIETY OPINIONS

Auditors render four types of opinions: Unqualified, Qualified, Adverse, and Disclaimer.

An *unqualified* opinion means the auditors concluded that the financial statements present fairly the company's financial results and financial positions in accordance with GAAP, not that the financial statements are 100 percent error free. The auditor is required to explain any exceptions to GAAP. This is the best opinion of all.

Qualified opinion means the auditors conclude that the financial statements are *not* presented fairly in accordance with GAAP. Perhaps the auditor was unable to perform a complete enough audit to render an unqualified opinion; accounting principles were not consistently applied from year to year, or uncertainties exist where the auditor cannot determine the likely effect on the company's financial position. Qualified opinions make it difficult to compare financial statements of different companies. Qualified opinions may signal impending trouble.

Adverse opinion means the auditors concluded that the financial statements as a whole are not prepared fairly in accordance with GAAP. An adverse opinion is a sign of trouble.

Disclaimer means the auditors are not expressing any opinion about the financial statements. Auditors may give a disclaimer because they feel they cannot make an adequate assessment of the company's financial position or there is a question as to whether the company will continue as an ongoing operation. A disclaimer is usually a warning sign of impending trouble.

In addition to these four types of opinions, the auditor's opinion may contain explanatory text that is added for emphasis.

In this lesson, you learned about the auditor's opinion. In the next lesson, you learn about owners' equity.

Owners' Equity

In this lesson, you learn about owners' equity.

Owners' equity includes preferred stock, common stock, additional paid in capital, retained earnings, treasury stock, foreign currency translation adjustment, and appropriated retained earnings.

> **Owners' Equity**   Owners' equity means the owners' stake in the company.

The Owners' Stake

Companies issue two general types of stock:

- *Preferred stock,* which represents ownership in a company but generally pays a fixed dividend every quarter or six months and carries no voting rights. Preferred stockholders are paid off after liability holders but before common stockholders. Preferred stock can be perpetual or have a stated maturity.

- *Common stock* represents ownership in a company— in effect, first loss in bad times and gains in good times.

ISSUING PREFERRED STOCK

Companies issue preferred stock to increase their equity and reduce their leverage. In addition, dividends on preferred stock and common stock are not tax deductible to the company paying the dividend. For companies that face relatively low tax rates, preferred stock can be an attractive funding source.

 Cumulative Preferred Dividends   Cumulative dividends means that all preferred stock dividends not paid must be paid before the company can pay any dividends to common stockholders.

Convertible preferred stock pays a periodic dividend and then the holder can convert the preferred stock into common stock at a specified conversion price.

COMMON STOCK—UPSIDE, DOWNSIDE

Common stock represents the residual interest in the company after the liabilities and preferred stock have been paid off. This means the common stockholders lose their money first in the event the company goes out of business.

Common stocks of established mature companies typically pay quarterly dividends. Management and the board of directors may increase dividends over time. If a company experiences financial trouble, it may cut the dividend to conserve cash.

 Voting Rights   If you own common stocks, exercise your shareholder's voting rights and take an active role in governing the company.

Additional Paid-in-Capital Additional paid-in-capital occurs when companies issue common stock and the proceeds from the sale of the common stock exceed the par value.

TREASURY STOCK

Treasury stock is shares of the company's common stock the company issued in the past and has repurchased. Companies may hold treasury stock and possibly reissue it in the future or retire the shares. The amount of the treasury stock held by the company is recorded as a reduction to stockholders' equity.

DIVIDENDS VERSUS REINVESTMENT

Dividends are distributions of net earnings to shareholders. Growth companies generally pay no dividends so that they can reinvest 100 percent of net income in the business to fuel the company's growth. Established companies generally pay out a portion of net income in the form of dividends to common stockholders after first paying preferred dividends and retain the remainder to reinvest in the business.

DIVIDEND PAYOUT RATIO

The dividend payout ratio is the percentage of earnings or earnings per share the company pays to common shareholders in dividends. The higher the dividend payout ratio, the less earnings the company keeps to reinvest in its business.

SEGREGATING RETAINED EARNINGS

Appropriated retained earnings are the retained earnings earmarked for a specific purpose, but when they are not an expense/liability. Appropriated means the common stockholders don't have free and clear claim on that portion of the company's retained earnings. An example of appropriated retained earnings is damages arising from litigation against the company. Generally, appropriated retained earnings have a negative impact on the company's financial position.

 Foreign Exchange   Foreign exchange is the translation of financial transactions conducted in a foreign currency (for example, British pounds or Japanese yen) into U.S. dollars.

FOREIGN EXCHANGE

Financial statements of U.S. companies are presented in U.S. dollars. But many U.S. companies sell their products in foreign countries and many of those financial transactions are conducted in the local currency of that country. Foreign currency amounts must be translated into U.S. dollars.

Generally, assets and liabilities of foreign subsidiaries are translated into U.S. dollars at end-of-period rates of exchange. Income, expense, and cash flows are translated into U.S. dollars at weighted-average rates of exchange for the period. The resulting currency transactions are totaled and reported as part of shareholders' equity.

In this lesson, you learned about owners' equity, including preferred and common stock. In the next lesson, you learn about the income statement.

THE INCOME STATEMENT

In this lesson, you learn about the income statement.

A GREAT YEAR

The income statement presents the results of the company's business operations for the relevant quarter or year.

Through the income statement, you can analyze how the company employs its assets to generate sales and the expenses they incur to operate their business. A handy tool is to compare the revenue and expense categories as a percent of sales. This helps you determine trends and analyze the company's progress. A growing company should report higher sales and higher income.

Sales Revenue   Sales revenue is the dollar value of the goods and services the company sells during the quarter or year. Remember the following formula:

Sales Revenue = Price × Quantity

Expenses   Expenses are costs incurred to generate sales and fund the company's operations.

WIN, LOSE, OR DRAW

Income Statement begins with sales revenue. Sales revenue equals the price of the goods sold multiplied by the quantity of goods sold. Sales revenue is recorded on the income statement net of returns.

ANALYZING TRENDS

Trend analysis is particularly important to consider when analyzing companies. It is worthwhile to calculate the sales growth from year to year. When you compare the sales activity for two successive years, you can gain a sense of how the company's business is developing.

Sales growth is calculated by taking the difference between two sales figures (1998 minus 1997) and dividing that number by the earlier year's (1997) sales. It is easier for a smaller company to achieve high sales growth than a larger company.

Changes in Sales   Sales will change from period to period based on changes in prices, volume of product sold, and the mix of products sold.

> **Declining Rates** Look for trends and changes in sales and the other income statement components. Beware of a declining rate of increase in sales.

EARNINGS PROCESS

Earnings process means the company has completed all steps and duties required to sell the goods or services to the customer and the company can reasonably determine that the customer will pay the bill. When the company completes the earnings process, it records sales revenue in its accounting books. This is either cash if the customer pays cash or accounts receivable if the customer pays on credit.

ACCOUNTING FOR UNEARNED REVENUE

Unearned revenue means the company collected a fee, for example, but has yet to provide the services associated with the contract. When the company provides the services, they will reduce the unearned revenue liability and recognize sales revenue.

Deferred Revenue or Unearned Revenue
Deferred revenue or unearned revenue is sales revenue where the company has not completed the earnings process.

LONG-TERM CONTRACTS REVENUE

Companies that construct major projects such as electric power plants and ships generally earn revenue under the installment method.

Generally, the customer will make progress payments every month based on certain milestones as construction progresses. And the construction agent will recognize a percentage of the profit in each period based on the percentage of the project completed.

INSTALLMENT METHOD

If the construction period extends beyond the agreed-upon period, and the construction agent faces cost overruns that it cannot pass on to its customer through higher prices—because of a fixed price contract—the construction agent would raise its cost of goods sold estimate and lower its gross profit. This would reduce the builder's earnings on this project.

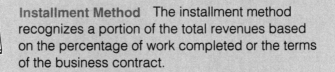

Installment Method   The installment method recognizes a portion of the total revenues based on the percentage of work completed or the terms of the business contract.

COMPLETED CONTRACT METHOD

A company follows the completed contract method when it is unsure of collecting the accounts receivable or there is a legal reason to defer recognizing the gross profit such as a material contingency regarding completion of the project.

Completed Contract Method   Completed contract method is when the company recognizes no gross profit during the construction period but defers the recognition of all the profit until the project is completed.

In this lesson, you learned about sales, returns, and other features of the income statement. In the next lesson, you learn about expenses.

Expenses—The Cost of Doing Business

In this lesson, you learn about different types of expenses.

Costs to Generate Sales and Run the Business

Expenses are costs a company incurs to generate sales and operate its business. Expenses are deducted from sales to arrive at taxable income. The most significant expense is typically cost of goods sold (COGS), which is the cost of the goods and services the company sells to its customers.

COGS includes:

- Cost of finished goods or inventory sold
- Factory overhead
- Direct labor

Companies often select LIFO inventory accounting for income tax purposes, which often results in higher tax deductions than FIFO inventory accounting. GAAP requires companies that use LIFO inventory accounting for income tax purposes to use LIFO for financial statement accounting purposes.

Factory Overhead   Factory overhead is the cost of operating the manufacturing plant.

Direct Labor   Direct labor is the wages and benefits the company pays to factory workers.

Factory overhead and direct labor are considered fixed costs because they are fixed-dollar amounts over certain levels of production. As discussed in Lesson 15, manufacturers add the cost of factory overhead and direct labor to work-in-process inventory, which eventually flows through COGS. So, increases in production volume tend to lower the average cost per unit of production.

PRODUCTION VARIABLES

As production volume rises and fixed overhead costs stay the same, profits should rise. At some production level, fixed costs will rise and profit may fall.

Super Retail can pay its workers overtime, which can be less expensive than hiring new employees and paying benefits. Similarly, a factory's capacity is fixed before the company has to expand the building and buy more machinery.

Profits also change based on the production quantity and the extent to which fixed overhead is spread over units of production and that lowers or raises average cost per unit. Profit changes based on the quantity of goods sold and the selling price.

Gross Profit   *Gross Profit Equals Sales – COGS.*
The greater the gross profit—the income available
to pay the company's other expenses—the more
profitable the company is likely to be.

OUTSIDE INFLUENCES

Outside events and factors such as economics, legal rulings,
and regulations influence the company you are analyzing.

In particular, you should beware of increasing inventory costs
and increasing cost of goods sold. A clothing store may face
rising costs if a drought ruins the cotton crop.

Big Margins   Look for companies with the high-
est profit margins in their industry and improving
profit margins. The more a company can increase
its profit margins, the more profitable it will be.

In this lesson, you learned about the different types of expenses. In the next lesson, you learn about other income statement items.

OTHER INCOME STATEMENT ITEMS

In this lesson, you learn about other income statement items.

COST OF MANAGEMENT AND DEBT

Two significant expense items are SG&A (selling, general, and administrative expenses) and interest expense.

Companies incur SG&A costs to pay nonmanufacturing costs such as managers' salaries and benefits, headquarters overhead, and salespeople's salaries and benefits. SG&A also includes other expense items that are incurred to operate the company, but not related to manufacturing its products. SG&A as a percent of sales equals SG&A expense divided by sales.

 Gauging Management   SG&A as a percent of sales may be used to gauge the efficiency of company management.

BORROWING MONEY

Interest expense is the cost of borrowing money, and is calculated as follows: Interest Expense = Debt Payable × Interest.

RISING INTEREST EXPENSE

Companies incur more debt and interest expense when they expand the business and also during a cash crunch. Rising interest expense, especially when sales and gross profit margins are not increasing, and when the company is not generating sufficient gross profit to cover its interest expense and other fixed charges, can be a sign of financial trouble.

Other Expenses   Other expenses is a term given to nonoperating costs and expenses that do not fit into the other income statement categories.

Gains   Gains arise from the sale of assets other than inventory, where the selling price exceeds the company's net book value in that asset.

Net Book Value   Net book value equals historical cost minus accumulated depreciation.

CALCULATING GAINS AND LOSSES

Gains occur when the selling price exceeds the net book value of the asset.

 Losses   Losses arise from the sale of assets other than inventory, where the selling price is less than the company's net book value in that asset.

In this lesson, you learned about various income statement items. In the next lesson, you learn about income from continuing operations and income taxes.

INCOME FROM CONTINUING OPERATIONS AND INCOME TAXES

In this lesson, you learn about income from continuing operations and income taxes.

BUSINESS PROFIT

Income from continuing operations equals income the company earns from its ongoing business activities and is shown on the income statement on a pretax basis (before income taxes).

CONFLICTING METHODS

In the United States, a company's GAAP accounting income statement almost always differs from its income statement prepared for U.S. income tax purposes because the rules for recording business transactions differ.

Tax Shield   Tax shield is the income tax savings generated by one dollar of income tax deduction. Tax shield represents an actual cash savings to the company because the company owes fewer taxes to the government.

Tax Shield = Tax Deduction × Tax Rate

Periodically, governments offer income tax credits to provide incentives to promote certain activities including Research and Development (R&D) and economic development in a particular region.

Tax Credit   Tax credit equals a dollar-for-dollar reduction in income taxes payable. Tax credits generally result in greater tax savings than tax deductions.

Deferred Taxes   Deferred taxes are the timing differences between income tax expense per the company's income tax return and income tax expense per the company's GAAP income statement.

DEFERRING TAXES

Deferred taxes arise from temporary or timing differences between income tax accounting for tax purposes and accounting purposes. These temporary differences are expected to reverse over time.

- Deferred tax liabilities arise when the company pays less income tax to the government than is due according to the GAAP income statement

- Deferred tax assets arise when the company pays more income tax to the government than is due according to the GAAP income statement

Deferred tax assets and liabilities are classified as long-term or short-term based on the expected reversal of the timing differences from the underlying asset or liability that gave rise to the deferred tax entry. Deferred tax balances are typically recorded on the balance sheet as:

- Net short-term deferred assets or liabilities

- Net long-term deferred assets or liabilities

In this lesson, you learned about income from continuing operations and income taxes. In the next lesson, you learn about other income statement items.

A Few More Income Statement Items

In this lesson, you learn about other income statement items, including discontinued operations.

Below the Line Income and Expenses

The income statement items explained in this lesson are recorded on the income statement below "net income from continuing operations," and these items are shown as "net of income taxes." Net of income taxes means income minus or loss plus income taxes. This treatment isolates nonrecurring activities and helps investors compare the results of continuing operations from year to year. Nonrecurring activities and events are one-time occurrences and are unlikely to be repeated.

Discontinuing Operations

Discontinued operations are business units, segments, or subsidiaries the company shuts down and for which it then plans to dispose of the assets. Discontinued operations means the discontinued business no longer is a part of the company's continuing operations.

Discontinued operations are shown on the income statement, net of income taxes. Income and loss related to discontinued operations typically appear on the income statement with two separate amounts:

- *Income or loss on operations.* Income or loss on operations is the net income or loss from operating the discontinued business.

- *Gain or loss on disposition.* Gain or loss on disposition is the estimated or actual loss or actual gain arising from the sale of the discontinued operation.

EXTRAORDINARY ITEMS

Extraordinary items are gains and losses that come from events outside the company's ordinary course of business. Extraordinary items are shown on the income statement as net of income taxes, similar to discontinued operations.

One example of an extraordinary item is gain or loss associated with the early retirement (extinguishment) of debt. Extinguishment debt is an extraordinary item because it is outside the scope of the company's ordinary business activities.

CUMULATIVE EFFECT OF CHANGE IN ACCOUNTING PRINCIPLE

Cumulative effect of change in accounting principle means the company switched from one accounting method to another. This income statement item reflects the company's total gain or loss arising from the change—as if the new accounting method had been implemented all along.

Changes in accounting principles come from switching from FIFO to LIFO inventory accounting and adjustment in pensions. Cumulative effect of changes in accounting principles are shown on the income statement, net of income taxes, similar to discontinued operations and extraordinary items.

In this lesson, you learned about discontinued operations, extraordinary items, and cumulative effect of change in accounting principle in income statements. In the next lesson, you learn about earnings per share.

EARNINGS PER SHARE

In this lesson, you learn about earnings per share (EPS) and price earnings multiples (p/e).

EARNINGS FOR COMMON STOCKHOLDERS

Earnings per share (EPS) is the net income earned by each share of common stock. To calculate EPS, divide net income available to common stockholders—after preferred stockholders have been paid—by weighted average number of shares of common stock outstanding.

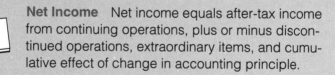

Net Income   Net income equals after-tax income from continuing operations, plus or minus discontinued operations, extraordinary items, and cumulative effect of change in accounting principle.

To calculate EPS, a company must consider the weighted average number of shares outstanding for the period—a quarter or year. Weighted-average means the number of shares outstanding for the period giving consideration to the amounts of time each share was outstanding.

IT WAS A GOOD OR BAD YEAR

Companies typically make two EPS calculations: Primary and Fully Diluted. The company is required to present both EPS calculations on the income statement.

 Primary EPS   Primary EPS is the EPS based on weighted-average shares of common stock and common stock equivalents, which are securities and other financial instruments that are convertible into shares of common stock.

Convertible securities include Convertible preferred stock, Convertible bonds, Rights, and Warrants.

When common stock equivalents are considered to be converted into common stock to calculate EPS, net income should be adjusted to reflect the concept that the company would not have to pay dividends on convertible preferred stock or interest on convertible debt if the securities were converted into common stock.

 Fully Diluted EPS   Fully diluted EPS means all common stock equivalents are considered to be converted into common stock.

 Rising Earnings   Look for a long-term trend of increasing EPS.

Price earnings (p/e) multiple means the current market price of the common stock divided by EPS.

> **!** **Too Big?**   Beware of companies where the p/e multiple greatly exceeds the EPS rate of growth. You may be overpaying for the company's growth.

In this lesson, you learned about earnings per share and p/e multiples. In the next lesson, you learn about the statement of cash flows.

STATEMENT OF CASH FLOWS

In this lesson, you learn about the Statement of Cash Flows.

CASH FROM THE BUSINESS

Statement of Cash Flows explains the differences between two consecutive balance sheets (for example, see Intel Corporation's for 1995, following) in terms of cash. Statement of Cash Flows is perhaps the most important financial statement because a company's ability to generate cash from operations is key to its future success.

TURNING SALES INTO CASH

Positive earnings does not necessarily mean the company is generating cash. For example, inventory and accounts receivable may increase, which in turn consumes cash.

The Statement of Cash Flows contains three activities: Operating, Investing, and Financing.

OPERATING ACTIVITIES

The Operating activities section begins with net income and contains adjustments to convert the net income into cash flow generated from operations.

 Operating Activities   Operating activities include all changes in balance sheet items that relate to the company's day-to-day business operations.

The Operating activities section usually includes three sections:

- Net earnings

- Adjustments to net income that neither use nor generate cash

- Changes in operating assets and liabilities

The first adjustments to net income are depreciation and amortization expense. These amounts are added back to net income because they were expenses but do not require cash outlays. The company spent cash when it purchased the asset or incurred the liability.

Changes in operating assets and liabilities include changes in current assets (except for cash) and current liabilities. Increases in accounts receivable and inventories are subtracted from net income because the company has more cash tied up (used) in these assets.

Consolidated Statements Of Cash Flows

Three years ended December 30, 1995

(In millions)	1995	1994	1993
Cash and cash equivalents, beginning of year	S 1,180	$ 1,659	$ 1,843
Cash flows provided by (used for) operating activities:			
Net income	3,566	2,288	2,295
Adjustments to reconcile net income to net cash provided by (used for) operating activities:			
Depreciation	1,371	1,028	717
Net loss on retirements of property, plant and equipment	75	42	36
Amortization of debt discount	8	19	17
Change in deferred tax assets and liabilities	346	(150)	12
Changes in assets and liabilities:			
(Increase) in accounts receivable	(1,138)	(530)	(379)
(Increase) in inventories	(835)	(331)	(303)
(Increase) in other assets	(241)	(13)	(68)
Increase in accounts payable	289	148	146
Tax benefit from employee stock plans	116	61	68
Increase in income taxes payable	372	38	32
Increase in accrued compensation and benefits	170	44	109
(Decrease) increase in other liabilities	(73)	337	119
Total adjustments	460	693	506
Net cash provided by operating activities	4,026	2,981	2,801
Cash flows provided by (used for) investing activities:			
Additions to property, plant and equipment	(3,550)	(2,441)	(1,933)
Purchases of long-term, available-for-sale investments	(129)	(975)	(1,165)
Sales of long-term, available-for-sale investments	114	10	5
Maturities and other changes in available-for-sale investments, net	878	503	(244)
Net cash (used for) investing activities	(2,687)	(2,903)	(3,337)
Cash flows provided by (used for) financing activities:			
(Decrease) increase in short-term debt, net	(179)	(63)	197
Additions to long-term debt	—	128	148
Retirement of long-term debt	(4)	(98)	—
Proceeds from sales of shares through employee stock plans and other	192	150	133
Proceeds from sale of Step-Up Warrants, net	—	—	287
Proceeds from sales of put warrants, net of repurchases	85	76	62
Repurchase and retirement of Common Stock	(1,034)	(658)	(391)
Payment of dividends to stockholders	(116)	(92)	(84)
Net cash (used for) provided by financing activities	(1,056)	(557)	352
Net increase (decrease) in cash and cash equivalents	283	(479)	(184)
Cash and cash equivalents, end of year	S 1,463	$ 1,180	$ 1,659
Supplemental disclosures of cash flow information:			
Cash paid during the year for:			
Interest	S 182	$ 76	$ 39
Income taxes	S 1,209	$ 1,366	$ 1,123

Cash paid for interest in 1995 includes approximately $108 million of accumulated interest on Zero Coupon Notes that matured in 1995.

See accompanying notes.

Cash Generation Efficiency Ratio   Cash generation efficiency ratio equals actual cash generated by operations per the Statement of Cash Flows divided by potential cash generated by operations.

One way to approximate potential cash flow is net income plus depreciation expense plus amortization expense. A cash generation efficiency ratio of less than 90 percent means the company may be experiencing difficulty converting its income from continuing operations into cash.

Investing Activities

Investing activities include purchases and sales of PP&E, mergers and acquisitions, and purchases of and sales from marketable securities.

Companies invest money to expand their business. They routinely buy new machinery, build new plants, and make capital expenditures. Companies also make investments in marketable securities. In addition, companies sell these assets to generate cash or free up cash for other investments.

Financing Activities

Financing activities describe how the company finances its business. They include the issuance, repayment and retirement of debt, preferred stock and common stock, and also the payment of dividends.

In this lesson, you learned about the Statement of Cash Flows. In the next lesson, you learn about additional tools for analyzing companies and annual reports.

MORE ANALYTICAL TOOLS

In this lesson, you learn about a few more tools that are useful for analyzing companies and annual reports.

ANALYZING RATIOS

As you've learned so far, annual reports and prospectuses contain a wealth of information for investors and other interested parties. This lesson describes a few additional tools that will help you determine a company's financial position.

RETURN ON ASSETS

Return on assets is how efficiently the company is using its assets in the business to generate sales. One measurement is how much net income the company generates from the average assets it employs. Return on Assets equals net income divided by average total assets.

Using Assets Productively   The higher the return on assets, the more productively the company is using its assets.

RETURN ON SALES

Investors gauge the success of the company in managing its expenses. One measure is return on sales. Return on sales is the percentage of sales that the company converts into profit, and is calculated as net income divided by sales.

In other words, for every dollar in sales, how much net income does the company generate?

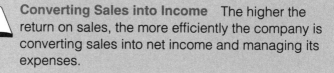 **Converting Sales into Income**   The higher the return on sales, the more efficiently the company is converting sales into net income and managing its expenses.

Rising sales is very important to a company's success, but the company's ability to generate cash from those sales is crucial. Cash pays the bills, services the debt, and pays the shareholders.

 Cash Available to Pay Interest   Cash available to pay interest means cash earnings before interest, depreciation and amortization, and income tax expenses.

MEASURING ABILITY TO PAY

Interest coverage and fixed-charge coverage ratios measure a company's ability to pay its fixed charges.

Interest coverage is how many times the company can pay its annual interest expense. This is calculated as cash earnings available to pay interest expense divided by annual interest expense.

 Comfort Level   An interest coverage ratio of at least 3 to 4 times is considered to provide reasonable assurance that the company can pay its interest expense.

FIXED-CHARGE COVERAGE

Fixed-charge coverage means how many times the company can pay its annual fixed charges. This ratio is calculated as cash available to pay fixed charges divided by annual fixed charges. Fixed charges means all fixed payments the company is required to make in the upcoming year. Fixed charges typically include:

- Debt service payments including principal and interest

- Minimum lease payments (rent)

- Royalty and license payments

- Take-or-pay contract amounts, which are obligations to buy a certain quantity of goods (usually natural resources) regardless of whether the company wants the goods or not

A fixed charge coverage ratio of at least 2–3 times assures that the company can pay its fixed charges.

Measuring Debt

Investors also calculate these two ratios to measure a company's leverage (debt):

- Debt-to-equity ratio
- Debt-to-total capital ratio

The calculation for debt-to-equity is total debt divided by total equity.

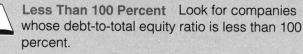 **Less Than 100 Percent**   Look for companies whose debt-to-total equity ratio is less than 100 percent.

The calculation for debt-to-total capital is total debt divided by total debt plus total equity.

Less Than Half   Look for companies whose debt-to-total capital ratio is less than 50 percent.

The amount of debt a company can service varies by company and industry and varies over time due to changes in the nature of the industry. Companies in industries that tend to be more cyclical and volatile may be less able to carry as much debt as a utility.

RETURN ON EQUITY

The calculation for return on equity is net income available to common stockholders divided by the average equity.

EFFECTIVE ANALYSIS

To conduct an effective analysis of a company, you must study companies and industries over a number of years. It is important to compare financial ratios of companies over successive periods to determine whether the company's results are improving or deteriorating. You should analyze external factors that affect the company, including economic, competitive, and regulatory forces.

You should study long-term trends in the financial statements including:

- Sales growth

- Gross profit margin

- Earnings and EPS

- Dividends and dividend growth

- Leverage (debt)

In this lesson, you learned about analytical tools that help you learn more about a company's financial condition.

The *10 Minute Guide to Annual Reports and Prospectuses* explained the information contained in annual reports and prospectuses. Each lesson described an aspect of financial analysis—in particular, how to interpret financial statements and other information the company discloses. By now, you've gained insight into investment decision making, and have become acquainted with the questions to ask before making an investment decision. The next lesson is up to you.

INDEX